COME FILL THIS PLACE

A Journey in Prayer

STACY DIETZ

KNOWLEDGE POWER BOOKS

Copyright © 2019 by Stacy Dietz
All rights reserved. In accordance with the U.S. Copyright Act of 1976, the scanning, uploading, and electronic sharing of any part of this book without the permission of the publisher is unlawful piracy and theft of the author's intellectual property. If you would like to use material from this book (other than for review purposes), prior written permission must be obtained by contacting the publisher at info@knowledgepowerinc.com

Thank you for your support of the author's rights.

ISBN: 978-1-950936-04-5 (Hardcover)
Library of Congress Control Number: 2019907379

ISBN: 978-1-950936-02-1 (Paperback)
ISBN: 978-1-950936-00-7 (E-book)

Library of Congress Control Number: Pending
Edited By: Steve Robinson, Julie Lewis
Cover Design: Juan Roberts, Creative Lunacy, Inc.
Interior Design: Jennifer Houle
Literary Director: Sandra L. Slayton

Unless otherwise indicated, Scripture quotations are from the Holy Bible, New International Version®. NIV®. Copyright © 1973, 1978, 1984, 2011 by Biblica, Inc.TM Used by permission of NavPress. All rights reserved. Represented by Tyndale House Publishers, Inc.

Scripture quotations identified The Message are from *The Message*. Copyright © by Eugene H. Peterson 1993, 1994, 1995, 1996, 2000, 2001, 2002. Used by permission of NavPress. All rights reserved. Used by permission. (www.Lockman.org)

Published by KP Publishing
A Division of Knowledge Power Communications, Inc.
Valencia, CA 91355
www.kp-pub.com
www.knowledgepowerinc.com

Printed in the United States of America

DEDICATION

God taught me to love and inspired me to live. He caught me unaware. This book is about the need for a relationship with Him through prayer, and so it is dedicated first, to God. Second, this book is dedicated to every wanderer who is looking for something bigger and better. For every person who feels ordinary and wants to be "extra" ordinary, look to God. He created you in His image (Genesis 1:27). To every person who feels lost, broken, forgotten, unworthy, or mistreated, but wants to be loved, He sent His son for you (Isaiah 61:1-3) because you are already loved (John 15:9). For every person who wants to live a meaningful life with purpose and supernatural guidance, look to Him, He sent a helper (John 14:26). Therefore I dedicate this book to those who need faith, hope, and love.

You are not alone.

COME FILL THIS PLACE

You Already Know Me—Psalm 139:1-10
You have searched me, Lord, and you know me.
You know when I sit and when I rise;
You perceive my thoughts from afar.
You discern my going out and my lying down;
you are familiar with all my ways.
Before a word is on my tongue you,
Lord, know it completely.
You hem me in behind and before,
and you lay your hand upon me.
Such knowledge is too wonderful for me,
too lofty for me to attain.
Where can I go from your Spirit?
Where can I flee from your presence?
If I go up to the heavens, you are there;
if I make my bed in the depths, you are there.
If I rise on the wings of the dawn,
if I settle on the far side of the sea,
Even there your hand will guide me;
your right hand will hold me fast.

INTRODUCTION

This book is not meant to be a "how to pray" book. Jesus has given us a model on how to pray. There is a section in this book that offers thoughts on the model Jesus has given us, but that is not the primary reason this book was written. It was written in hope that you will start your own journey in prayer by sharing what I have learned on my journey.

Jesus taught on many things that are significant for our lives both now and for eternity. Many of those lessons are meaningful and impactful to our prayers. Prayer cannot be simplified into a formula, and I certainly cannot model it any better than Jesus.

Our relationship with God is dynamic, spiritual, and evolving. The words written here are fundamentally about the need for prayer. It is meant to be a reaching out through my story, the wisdom of others, along with God's Word in hope that you invite God into your own life journey.

By using my own life as an example, in addition to what I have gleaned from scripture and other influences, I hope to inspire others to invigorate their spiritual journey through prayer. Each person's journey is unique, personal, and very intimate.

"The Spirit himself bears witness to our spirit that we are children of God" (Romans 8:16). We can interact with God's spiritual nature because we were initially created to abide with Him in the Garden of Eden. Although we now live in a broken world, our connection to God is not lost. God's own Spirit lives in us and is active in our lives.

Just as with any relationship that we hope to nurture, we must interact daily with those to whom we wish to connect. This book is about inspiring others to choose to connect with God rather than the false spiritual connections in this world. This book is also about encouraging people to find out, for themselves, the difference between God's truth and Satan's deception.

CONTENTS

Dedication	v
Introduction	vii
Chapter 1: Persistence and Perseverance	1
Chapter 2: Pride	13
Chapter 3: God's Economy	25
Chapter 4: Our Hearts and Motives	31
Chapter 5: Why Pray? Pivotal Event	41
Chapter 6: God Is Supernatural—We're Not!	51
Chapter 7: Spiritual Warfare	57
Chapter 8: Holy Spirit	71
Chapter 9: We Have a Model—The Lord's Prayer	83
Chapter 10: *Ask, Seek,* and *Knock*	101
Acknowledgments	121
Notes	123
Appendix	129
About the Author	159

CHAPTER 1

PERSISTENCE AND PERSEVERANCE

"Success is no accident. It is hard work, perseverance, learning, studying, sacrifice and most of all, love of what you are doing or learning to do."
—Pele

"Once you learn to quit, it becomes a habit."
—Vince Lombardi Jr.

When I paint or draw, I tend to really examine what I'm going to copy. I spend time trying to notice all the little color changes and shapes, anything that will help me recreate my subject matter as best as I can.

This is a lot like faith or, rather, incorporating faith into action. If I'm trying to be the best version of who God created me to be, then looking at Him would help me know what He would create and what I'm meant to do. It's a bit of a circle, but it helps simplify how to live my life.

If I would like my life to reflect my Maker, then it makes sense to really look at who He is—all the little nuances and all the character traits. I do this by reading about Him which causes me to notice Him just about anywhere. The key is recognizing Him.

Much like an artist, God has His own style. He is the Creator of life (Genesis 1:1, Job 33:4, Proverbs 22:2, Jeremiah 23:24, Isaiah 40:28). There are certain things He would and wouldn't do. For instance, God won't break a promise (Psalm 89:34). God will not abandon you (Deuteronomy 31:6). God doesn't stop loving you (Jeremiah 31:3). Who God is, and what is important to Him are important to know as we progress in our journey with Him. In addition to our own limitations, there are forces that try to deter us from getting to know who God is, to keep us from recognizing His voice and to keep us from inviting Him into our lives. The journey is worthwhile because our lives become so enriched when He is involved.

Recently I went to Hawaii and spent time with my extended family. Over the course of this time, I had some experiences that rekindled my interest in putting my thoughts down on paper. I value the people in my life now (and initially looked for "something" to get me through difficult times) because of previous experiences in my early adulthood. The root of what I experienced and what motivated me is simple: some of the people in my life disappointed and hurt me, and I, too, have hurt and disappointed others. I felt broken and made bad decisions because of that brokenness.

The problem is, when I went back to Hawaii and was immersed in my cultural roots, I felt like I was going backwards. I was thinking things and seeing things that caused me to revisit the years when I felt broken. I remembered what it was like when I was not making good choices.

That was my past, and I wanted to leave it there, as far away as possible. For over twenty-five years, my in-laws represented family to me, living life as best they can in accordance with their faith. They are imperfect, yet they balance honesty and consideration, caring for others while acknowledging boundaries that don't cause resentment. They work hard, love deeply, and look for the best in people. They have a healthy skepticism that keeps them searching for their own answers for the questions they have.

I have lived with this wonderful balance of big personalities, each with their individual opinions that are honestly stated with a healthy dose of love while looking out for each other and doing what is right. Agree or disagree, but at the end of the day, it's ok to be yourself. We hold each other accountable without judgment, and I am grateful for that.

For over twenty-five years, and often times by their example rather than their words, my in-laws have taught me how to be a better parent and inspired to me to be a more compassionate person. Although I am quite different, I have found a comfortable place among my husband's rather large family. With them, I feel safe and accepted in spite of our differences. I am held accountable for the faith I choose to follow. They are authentic; their "yes" means "yes" and their "no" means "no." They don't offer what they don't have, they don't take what they didn't earn, and they don't say what they don't mean. You are who you are, and they are who they are. There can be passionate, opinionated discussions, yet at the end of the day, they are responsible for their thoughts and actions, and I am responsible for mine. I have found immense comfort in this.

This particular trip to Hawaii seemed to expose some of the residual triggers from my youth and early adulthood. I had grown up motivated by fear and often felt unworthy. This trip was also different because my husband and children were absent, and somehow the insecurities and sense of unworthiness I felt as a young person surfaced. Feelings of inadequacy and the fear of failure often kept me from pursuing my dreams.

Late one night in the midst of this trip, I felt desperate to have a conversation that reminded me of who God is and to hear someone who loved Him speak about Him. Shortly before this trip, I had given a little teaching to a small group of women about relationships and how God wants us to live in community. Even He lives in community, God (the Father), Jesus (the Son), and the Holy Spirit.

That day it was too late to call my husband because of the time difference. As I thought about the principals I shared about living in community, I made a decision that was a game changer for this trip. I phoned my uncle who lives on the island

and whom I have not called before. My uncle did remind me of who God is, and it was refreshing at a very deep level to hear words he had memorized because of his faith. My uncle also reminded me that I am living my life for God. This book is His, and that's whose opinion I should be concerned with. He instructed me to find a rock, write the "opala" in my heart (the Hawaiian word for trash), and take it to the ocean and throw it away. Casting anxiety and cares to God is biblical (1 Peter 5:7, Psalm 55:22, Isaiah 2:20). He told me to go and look for a rock to write on, telling me I would just "see" it.

I prayed that I could find a word, specific and concise, that would represent the things that most hinder me. The next trip to the beach, while standing on the curb waiting for my cousin to park her car after unloading our beach gear, my eyes found a smooth black rock, and I grabbed it. I realized I had nothing to write with and figured the blackness of the rock could represent the blackness of the "opala" I was told to throw away.

It was perfect.

Minutes later while in my lounge chair, I sat and prayed, quietly asking God to show me everything in my heart that needed to be thrown away. While doing this, I glanced to the side of my chair, and on the sand, spotted a white, pitted, very imperfect stone. It reminded me of what I thought of myself: unworthy, a little dinged up, definitely not perfect. But it was white. The whiteness of it was to my liking and reminded me of God. I want my life to be so filled with Him that people see all the whiteness that belongs to Him despite all the pits that belong to me. It was not perfect, and I am far from perfect, but to me, that little white pitted rock represented how God can do amazing things for—and through—imperfect people who don't seem or feel worthy. Moses is a great example of this. He led a nation out of Egypt even though he felt unworthy and was slow of speech (Exodus 3:11, 4:10-12). Not only did God set up the circumstances where a powerful Pharaoh would let a nation of slaves leave, but they would not leave Egypt empty-handed (Exodus 3:19-22, 6:1). The Egyptians were plundered because God made the Egyptians favorably disposed to His people. The women just asked for articles of silver and gold and for clothing which they put on their sons and daughters who wore those riches to freedom!¹

I grabbed this rock and knew this represented freedom for me. I wanted to go home free.

So what was it that kept me from feeling free? I looked at the black rock and knew that the root of so many of my anxious ways stemmed from fear. Fear of failure, fear of not being good enough, fear of not being chosen, fear of being left behind, fear of being abandoned, on and on the thoughts came through the open floodgates of my mind. I had prayed that God would *"search me and know my anxious ways"* (Psalm 139:23). He would show me a word that could be attached to that black rock and thrown into the ocean. He did exactly that but so much more, as well, just as He did for the Egyptians, and as He does when He is involved in our lives, He makes them so much more.

Another thing my uncle asked me to do was to look around at the moment I threw the rock in the ocean and soak in what was before my eyes. I floated on a boogie board, ready to cast my little black "opala" rock into the sea, and then turned to look back to shore, as my uncle had asked. My cousin was there, and she looked as she did as a young girl, running with boogie board in hand, laughing and being free. She hadn't looked that free since we were young together, on this island, playing in the ocean. We are like sisters, and in that moment, I was grateful God let me see her free. Then further, onto the sand, was her sister, my other cousin, sitting on a chair under an umbrella, watching out for us as she always does. She was an anchor in that moment, reminding me that God is an anchor for me.

I turned around and looked at the water surrounding me. Not naturally an explorer at heart, I do venture out spiritually, especially for those I care for and love even if it means I have to extend myself into places where I don't feel safe. I'll do it anyway for them. God is bigger than me and I cannot completely know everything about Him or how He works. This was how the ocean appeared to me just then: big, uncertain, and exciting. I happily followed my uncle's advice and threw the stone.

COME FILL THIS PLACE

With freedom in mind, I decided to retry something I had sheepishly attempted a few days earlier, but had been too worried about how it looked to even give it more than a few tries. It was simple; I wanted to sit on the boogie board. With legs flying, arms flailing, and what I imagined to be unflattering views of me falling off the board, I gave up easily. Now after throwing my "opala" rock into the ocean, what others thought of me didn't matter as much. Like the thoughts regarding others' opinions of me even before I came to Hawaii, who even knows what anyone is thinking? It's more likely they don't even notice me among the many active people in the ocean. So with determination, I decided I would try again without fearing what strangers or others thought of me.

Trying to sit on a boogie board is a lot like following God. It takes persistence, relaxation, and the willingness to be in harmony with your surroundings. In this case, it was the movement of the ocean around me. I improved and eventually did enjoy some time floating in the beautiful ocean learning about God and my journey with Him. Like the ocean, He moves the way He wants, and I must trust (relax) and move with Him. Focusing on Him, just as I had to focus on the ocean helped me to persevere.

After my trip was over and I returned home, I shared some of my thoughts with my eldest daughter about my time in Hawaii. We began discussing ideas for my book. Writing has always been a project on the back burner for many years. For so long I had let fear of the unknown get in the way of me doing something that I had always dreamt of doing.

My daughter is a very intelligent young lady. She majored in English and graduated from UCLA with top honors before continuing on to medical school. She asked me a simple question, "What is failure to you?"

"Not getting it published."

"That's interesting," she said, "because I see failure as not writing."

Immediately, I'm back in the ocean in Hawaii, remembering that freedom is not being bound by fear. My perspective was warped! I had lived with the perspective that was entangled with a fear of being rejected, of not being good enough, of worrying how I looked to people. This had become a habit that I knew I was going to have to break.

While my daughter and I continued our chat, I reminisced about the way I felt on the ocean after throwing my "opala" rock. My perspective had shifted thus freeing me all while floating on a boogie board! Correcting my habitual way of thinking is a process that continues, so I am grateful that God has given me another day to persist, to try, to learn, and to be free. Like the pitted white stone, my journey may be covered with imperfections, but my prayer is that "freedom" will be stamped over everything that I'm meant to do.

> *"For My thoughts are not your thoughts, nor are your ways My ways," declares the Lord. "For as the heavens are higher than the earth, so are My ways higher than your ways and my thoughts than your thoughts"* (Isaiah 55:8-9).

If God's ways are more than we can comprehend, then how can we know and accomplish His will? Persistence is one of the keys. We have to keep taking the steps we are able to take. God left us a great treasure map in the Bible. There are many places to hunt for the treasure He wants us to discover. Everyone is on their own independent and personal journey with God. Most of us live both in community and independently of each other. We are at different places in our journeys, each walking in our own shoes. We each have our own questions for God. We each have our own relationship with God. Our life experiences are unique; our personalities, goals, passions, and abilities are unique. We are different, yet we are all called to a common purpose. 1 Corinthians 12:12 talks about this very issue:

> *"Just as a body, though one, has many parts, but all its many parts form one body, so it is with Christ." It continues in verses 15-20: "Now if the foot should say, "Because I am not a hand, I do not belong to the body," it would not for that reason stop being part of the body. And if the ear*

should say, "Because I am not an eye, I do not belong to the body," it would not for that reason stop being part of the body. If the whole body were an eye, where would the sense of hearing be? If the whole body were an ear, where would the sense of smell be? But in fact God has placed the parts in the body, every one of them, just as He wanted them to be. If they were all one part, where would the body be? As it is, there are many parts, but one body."

We are different and yet we have a common goal. We need to use our own uniqueness, talents, and gifts to move together to accomplish "something." That "something" has to do with what God finds important. Before we go out and "do something" with our unique gifts and talents, and before we join with others to do "anything," maybe we should know what comes before everything else.

Jesus talks about this (Mark 12) after finishing a debate with some Sadducees (members of an ancient Jewish group of priests and aristocrats)[2] about the afterlife. A scribe (or teacher of the law)[3] comes along, hears them debating, and asks Jesus which of all the commandments is the most important? In other words, what is the most important thing we are to do? Of all the things taught to us in the Bible, what does God want us to do, first and foremost? This is the answer Jesus gives (Mark 12:29-31):

"Love the Lord your God with all your heart and with all your soul and with all your mind and with all your strength. The second is this: Love your neighbor as yourself. There is no commandment greater than these."

So how do we walk that journey towards God? Love comes first. Specifically, loving God and loving others. Isn't it a wonder we are all searching for Love?! Just like that song, we may be searching for love in all the wrong places, but one thing is true, we are made to love.

Prayer is fundamental to loving. It's fundamental to loving my neighbor as myself. Truthfully, it would be great to love my neighbor as much as I love even my family, but this is a struggle for me. This absolutely takes a lot of prayer!

Many years ago, we moved into a house with a view overlooking some mountains. It was a new neighborhood so many people were adding on to their houses, customizing each to their own needs. Our neighbor built a very large two-story garage that blocked most of our view from our backyard area near the house, and I was not feeling "love" for my neighbor. I stewed and got upset, focusing on the view that had been lost until my husband said something simple and yet perspective-changing for me. He mentioned that just like we felt God gave us our dream home, perhaps He gave our neighbor his dream home, as well, and that it just included a monster garage. Instead of focusing on the view I had lost, which would have caused problems between neighbors, why didn't I just walk up the hill on the back half of the property and look at the incredible view that was still there? Loving my neighbor included wanting him to have the desires of his heart even if it requires sacrifice from me. If we had bought our house after our neighbor had built his garage, I never would have even complained!

In Colossians 3:12-14, we are asked to treat others a specific way:

> *"Therefore, as God's chosen people, holy and dearly loved, clothe yourselves with compassion, kindness, humility, gentleness, and patience. Bear with each other and forgive one another if any of you has a grievance against someone. Forgive as the Lord forgave you. And over all these virtues put on love, which binds them all together in perfect unity."*

I love this picture, being adorned with all these beautiful qualities. Choosing to "put on" compassion, kindness, humility, gentleness, and patience touches my heart deeply. It's something I want to do all the time and yet, sadly, don't. It's through asking for these things daily (at times, every minute!) that I am able to let the Holy Spirit work in my life. For those who question their purpose in life, here is a purpose that has been divinely given and will be eternally rewarded.

It is repeated in another part of the Bible. Luke 10:25-27 describes it:

> *"On one occasion an expert in the law stood up to test Jesus. "Teacher," he asked, "what must I do to inherit eternal life?" In verse 27: "Jesus answered, "Love the Lord your God with all your heart and with all your soul and with all your strength and with all your mind; and, love your neighbor as yourself.""*

So simple, love God with all our heart, with all our soul, and with all our strength, and love our neighbor as much as we love ourselves. Although it sounds simple, how can we love like we are asked to love? Our natural instincts are not to put our neighbor's needs above our own, and how do we love God so purely and passionately that it is done with every ounce of our being? I believe the key is praying and to pursue God with persistence. Recently, in an effort to find inspiration in conquering my lifelong struggle regarding my weight, I searched the web for quotes that could be taped to my mirror in hopes of being reminded daily that I could beat this longtime enemy. These are just a few quotes from anonymous sources that I found:

"Some people dream about success . . . while others wake up and work hard at it."

"Success is achieved and maintained by those who try—and keep trying."

"Everyday is a good day to SUCCEED!"

"If at first you don't succeed—try, try again."

"Persevere, and you will win the prize."

Although my weight issue is wrapped up with so many other issues, the realization that the key to success in anything, anything at all, is perseverance became clear. It's not just relegated to spiritual issues; it's a "truth." This truth is universal, and it's important to every aspect of our lives.

Persistence and Perseverance

In Luke 18:2-5 it says:

> *"Jesus tells his disciples a parable to show them that they should always pray and not give up. He said: "In a certain town there was a judge who neither feared God nor cared what people thought. And there was a widow in that town who kept coming to him with the plea, 'Grant me justice against my adversary.' For some time he refused. But finally he said to himself, 'Even though I don't fear God or care what people think, yet because this widow keeps bothering me, I will see that she gets justice, so that she won't eventually come and attack me!'" Verse 6 continues: "And the Lord said, "Listen to what the unjust judge says. And will not God bring about justice for his chosen ones, who cry out to him day and night? Will he keep putting them off?'"*

What is being pointed out here is that if the unjust judge will give the widow what she wants because of her persistence, how much more will our loving, caring God give you? Not only is our God able, He is willing. Our persistent pursuit of God and our persistent prayers will bring answers, provision, and wisdom. What we seek, we will find, and we will not fail if we do not give up! Our journey isn't about perfection; it's about persistence.

In Ephesians 6:18, after a description of our spiritual armor, we are asked to always keep on praying for all the Lord's people. Not only are we to pray for ourselves, but we are asked to persistently pray for others, as well. It is a great comfort of mine to know that we are bonded in our prayers. We can protect each other, we can petition for each other, and we can help one another through our prayers for each other. One of the shortest verses in the Bible about prayer is found in 1 Thessalonians 5:17. It simply says, *"pray continually."* It isn't written, "pray perfectly," it's written, *"pray continually."* One of the keys to a rich prayer life is simply to pray with persistence.

CHAPTER 2

PRIDE

*"A proud man is always looking down on things and people;
and, of course, as long as you are looking down, you cannot
see something that is above you."*
—C.S. Lewis, Mere Christianity

*"It was pride that changed angels into devils; it is humility
that makes men as angels."*
—St. Augustine

When we pray, it does matter what kind of attitude we have if we want God to answer us (James 4:2-3). More importantly, our prayers are a place where we can build a relationship with God.

Webster's dictionary defines pride simply as inordinate self-esteem. Closely related words are arrogance, exalt, and conceit.[1] This way of thinking focuses internally and hinders focusing on who God is and what He would like to give to you.

The near opposite of pride is something God values tremendously and will reward greatly; it is humility (Proverbs 22:4). Humility is described as being modest and unassuming, which includes having an attitude that does not put yourself above others.[2] That means being arrogant, entitled, egotistical or feeling deserving of things over another, is contrary to the model Jesus exemplified for us and is not something God condones.

Society as a whole doesn't value humility, submission, deference, or modesty. First and foremost we are about our rights. I'm not addressing political views or human rights stolen from one another in this book. If everyone was living with an attitude of deference and humility, no one would need to fight for their rights. Everyone would be valued and cherished as God intended. It's our feeling entitled and a desire to primarily focus on our own desires that can rob another of something they need. This is a huge issue to be tackled on another platform. The humility I'm speaking of is in relation to God.

A great place to start your faith journey and deepen your prayer life is by getting to know who God is. This happens by reading about Him (in the Bible), being in community (with others), and also through life experiences. Sometimes it's like a courtship, and at times it's like research, but if you do not know the character of God, it can be hard to put your faith in Him. Although God cannot be completely and concisely described, here are some attributes that can help describe the character of God:[3,4,5]

SOVEREIGN: Independent; self-governing and not ruled by another entity. With complete power and authority. Outstanding
(Exodus 18:11, Psalm 115:3, Ephesians 1:11).

TRANSCENDENT: Superior in quality or achievement. Beyond limits of His creation. Independent of the world
(Isaiah 55:8-9, John 8:23, Psalm 113:5-6, Genesis 1:3-5).

ETERNAL: He is not finite; He has no beginning or end.
(Psalm 102:12, Psalm 90:2).

LOVE: An intense feeling of deep affection. (In Christian belief) the mercy, grace, and charity shown by God to humanity
(1 John 4:8, 16).

HOLY: Awe-inspiring. Consecrated. Sacred; a divine being or power
(Exodus 3:5-6, 1 Samuel 2:2, Psalm 99:2-3, Isaiah 6:3, Revelations 4:8).

OMNISCIENT: All-knowing
(Psalm 147:5, Acts 15:18, Romans 11:33, 1 John 3:20, Hebrews 4:13, Romans 2:16).

OMNIPOTENT: All powerful; possessing complete, unlimited, or universal power and authority
(Psalm 147:5, Acts 15:18, Romans 11:33, 1 John 3:20, Hebrews 4:13, Romans 2:16).

FAITHFUL: Consistently loyal, especially to a person, promise, or duty. Conscientious. Accurate and true. Reliable; can be trusted and relied upon
(Exodus 34:6, Deuteronomy 7:9, Revelations 3:14).

IMMUTABILITY: Unchanging
(Malachi 3:6, James 1:17, Hebrews 13:8).

In my journey to find God, I had many conversations with others, and many of them were helpful. I also read books, and some of those were insightful. Over the years I've concluded that there are many people who have opinions about who God is. One important principle that has served me very well, no matter what people tell me or what I read, is that it is very important to know who you are believing or listening to. "Know your source," was a mantra that I learned in a class on logical thinking.

The Bible is the word of God, written by men but inspired by God.[6] The Bible is my bottom line, and I try to make decisions and act according to what is written. I also learn a lot from others who share what they know about God. Yet, even these things will always be measured against who the Bible says God is. Of course, interpreting the bible is open to human error. God's Word is truth, but my understanding may be flawed. With this in mind, prayer and time spent with God through the Holy Spirit helps refine my understanding and better interpret truth. In prayer, it is helpful to have an open mind to revelations that facilitate a better understanding of God's character and purpose. He knows we aren't perfect, and that is certainly true of me. But God isn't asking for perfection. Only He is perfect.[7] He is asking us to be humble, to love, and to seek Him.

In my early twenties, I worked as a waitress at a local restaurant in the evening after spending all day at my day job. I worked many night shifts and spent a lot of time chatting after closing hours. It was there that I met a younger guy named Steve, who was a great listener and spoke to me in a way that didn't feel like judgment. We would just talk and share bits and pieces of our lives. Through this friendship, and through his brother Greg, who also worked at the restaurant, a door was opened into their family's life.

Greg and Steve were two of six siblings. They had a big family. Some of them I had previous connections with, and some I slowly got to know. Like a hawk, I watched how this family treated one another. Don't people live double lives? I thought this was true of everyone. That's how my life was lived. It was a skill that was honed, living a compartmental life: acting one way with one group of friends while acting another way with a different group of friends.

His family was intriguing. I'm sure they noticed that I said I believed in God but definitely did not walk with Him, not even close. The more time I spent with them, the more I noticed how honestly they lived. They were true to their beliefs, they were open about what they believed, and they were honest in how they treated others.

As I watched, two things became clear to me; God and family. They were not perfect, but in everything they did they measured themselves according to God and His Word. I kept looking for the lies, the secrets, or something they were hiding, because it was foreign to me that people could really live this way. If I just stuck around long enough and looked hard enough, flaws would materialize.

However, as time passed, I wanted what they had: peace and trust in something bigger than themselves. I wondered if their faith, peace, and trust in God would crumble when life knocked them down. How would they act when they didn't get what they wanted from God and when life didn't go their way?

My good friend, Steve, died at the age of nineteen. This was the moment when they demonstrated what their faith meant to them. His mother, Jane, despite her incredible sadness, thanked God for the gift He had given them for nineteen years. I was looking for bitterness or anger, maybe a well-deserved temper tantrum. Amidst their tragedy, they showed gratefulness and trust, in spite of their horrible loss. God was in their house that day, and I wanted what they had because it was real.

Faith is not something you can hold in your hand and tangibly pass on to someone else. But on that day, because of what this family honestly stood for, my life changed. I wanted peace through tragedy and sadness. I didn't deserve it, but I wanted something I could hold onto when everything came crashing down. Bad days would come, but I wanted a survival plan that was perfect. I wanted to hope for something better, something that would never fail me. So on that day in their kitchen, I gave my life to God. I no longer wanted to be the driver of my reckless and selfish journey; I wanted Him to make it something better than what I had made of it.

We make decisions in our everyday lives that require little leaps of faith because we trust the word of a friend or someone we find trustworthy. Eventually, no matter how much information we gather about God, no matter what people say about Him, just because of the nature of His supernatural being, we will eventually have to decide to trust that He is who He says He is. We will have to choose to spiritually jump towards an entity that does not operate entirely in our realm of understanding. While it is very valuable to our faith to know who He is, we cannot completely understand God because of how much less than Him we are. We will need a leap of faith.[8] Faith consists of trusting what you have reason to believe is true. As Moreland & Craig write in their book, *Philosophical Foundations for a Christian Worldview,* "It is not a blind, irrational leap into the dark."[9]

If you are a fan of extreme sports and have seen people free running or doing parkour, you would have a good picture of a literal leap of faith. They run and leap often while twisting, flipping, and rolling. Their leaps are unimaginable for the normal person. American Ninja Warriors are some of my favorite athletes to watch. They compete against one another on obstacle courses designed to challenge their physical and mental abilities. These courses, literally, require these athletes to take physical leaps of faith. They have to trust in themselves, their physical abilities and trust that their feet and hands will connect with something solid that will support them and further them in the course.

Spiritually, our leaps of faith are like those athletes. Their leaps of faith are connected to their physical abilities, but spiritually, our leaps of faith are connected to God's abilities. It is trust in knowing we will land where we need to and He will give us what we need so that we can accomplish what we need to do. We will be able to complete our own personal obstacle course of life, not because of who we are, but because of who He is. It requires trust not in our own abilities but in God's. Extreme-sport athletes often make blind landings, and our faith is like that as well.

Trusting God doesn't mean we will understand everything about who He is. It's good to investigate, ask questions, and search. In fact, He asks us to do that, but because of our intellectual and emotional limitations, making leaps of faith in our spiritual lives as well as our relationship with God, is necessary. Spiritual leaps of faith can be as exciting and inspiring as the physical leaps made by extreme-sport athletes. Although these athletes physically fly through the air, it is prayer that can bridge the unseen gap between us and God.

Spiritually, prayer connects us to where we physically cannot be connected. It helps us with our spiritual "leaps of faith." God is a supernatural being, we are natural beings of this physical world, and prayer is a conduit of sorts to a relationship with Him.

My first prayers were just a calling to Him, and it felt like a little tiny voice calling out in the dark. Had I been content to rely on my own efforts, to continue to shape my life as I saw fit, my pride would have kept me from so many wonderful experiences. Had I continued to focus on my own abilities to try to get the things I wanted for myself, I would have missed out on so much. Looking to God requires an outward perspective, towards Him and others. Although we focus inwardly at times, to focus primarily on our own needs above all else diminishes the impact God can have on our lives and through us, the lives of others.

Many times, people have said that they received so much more than they expected when they were helping another person accomplish something. Thinking of others and sacrificing things we want personally to help others succeed can be extremely rewarding. This may be contrary to what society suggests and to what most people believe but living my life surrendered to God has been far more rewarding than living it entirely for my own pleasure. Hearts, minds, and souls given to God with a spirit of deference or submission would be revolutionary for sure. Who in this current generation wants to submit to anyone? Biblical submission is not the same type of submission that is typically described by society. Rather, living in deference to God is living with an understanding that God is sovereign in all things.[10] God has a completely different economy from the world we live in. We find financial security, celebrity status, job titles, and material possessions—all valuable but those are not high on His list. He finds things like what He calls the "fruit of the spirit" valuable (Galatians 5:22-23):

> *"But the fruit of the Spirit is love, joy, peace, patience, kindness, goodness, faithfulness, gentleness, and self-control; against such things there is no law."*

Who doesn't want to have some of that? Yet, pride and entitlement would ensure that these are not given to others. If we cannot give, how can we expect to get? Even in our society, whether you believe in God or not, you have heard the word karma and understand the idea of getting what you do or don't deserve. Thankfully God does not deal in karma or giving us what we deserve.

God seems to be a stickler about a prideful heart, and this is a huge stumbling block to many of us. Part of the problem is that seeing God and acknowledging His work in our lives often occur when we reach our own limitations. If we cannot focus on anything but ourselves, our desires, and satisfying our own needs, we cannot focus on what God would like us to see. If we think we earn everything we attain, we cannot see what God has given us.

Pride is a stumbling block partly because it blinds us to God's blessings and provision. We glorify ourselves by making idols of our efforts, accomplishments, and even wisdom instead of God. People have a long history of creating their own idols; trying to create a god that fits their needs.[11] Pride can infiltrate our prayer life, robbing us of really seeking God in an effort to elevate ourselves and our own needs. Matthew 6:7 says:

> *"And when you pray, do not keep on babbling like pagans, for they think they will be heard because of their many words. Do not be like them, for your Father knows what you need before you ask him."*

This isn't about refraining from using a lot of words, but rather Jesus is saying don't babble; don't utter nonsense for the sake of sounding spiritual. Prayer isn't about sounding spiritual; it's about honest conversation. He's saying don't be prideful; don't babble trying to make ourselves look good.

God is not concerned with the words we utter as much as He is concerned with what our hearts desire and where we look for our treasure (Ecclesiastes 11:9). Romans 8:26-27 tells us that the *"Holy Spirit intercedes for us through wordless groans."* Even in the most accurate communication between us and God, words aren't needed. God is concerned with where our focus is, what draws our eyes and our attention. As parents, we often do the same thing. How much do we love when our children are being kind and considerate, taking care of each other, looking out for each other? How much of a relief is it when they aren't bickering and grabbing things for themselves? How much more do we want to give them when they are generous and share what they have and are grateful for what has already been given to them?

Almost everyone has heard of Satan. God created a most beautiful and powerful angel, yet instead of being grateful and instead of giving credit to his Maker, Satan wanted all eyes on himself. Therefore his sin was pride and selfish ambition (Ezekiel 28:17).[12] This is akin to plagiarism—stealing someone else's idea and refusing to give them credit for what they have created. Satan wanted to take God's work and claim it as his own. A piece of artwork cannot tell its artist it wasn't made by his or her hands and take credit for what it is. Also, something created specifically for one purpose cannot be used for something else. A painting cannot be a vase; a statue cannot be a waterfall. We are all given gifts from God, and He wants us to use them in a specific way. We aren't given things just for the sake of having them. We are all His children, and He wants us to share!!

> *"For by the grace given me I say to every one of you: Do not think of yourself more highly than you ought, but rather think of yourself with sober judgment, in accordance with the faith God has distributed to each of you. For just as each of us has one body with many members, and these members do not all have the same function, so in Christ we, though many, form one body, and each member belongs to all the others. We have different gifts, according to the grace given to each of us. If your gift is prophesying, then prophesy in accordance with your faith; if it is serving, then serve; if it is teaching, then teach; if it is to encourage, then give encouragement; if it is giving, then give generously; if it is to lead, do it diligently; if it is to show mercy, do it cheerfully"* (Romans 12:3-8).

Satan didn't want to share anything he was given. He wanted to covet, to keep, and to take something that wasn't his. How silly is it that a painting would take credit for its beauty? How silly is it that a son or daughter would take credit for their looks when their mother and father gave them the genes that created their bodies? Satan wants us to be like him, in that way. He works so hard to keep us from knowing who God is, and to prevent us from seeing Him and understanding how much God loves us. He wants us to take credit for what we earn, he wants us to take credit for what is given to us, and he wants us to feel entitled. He wants us looking anywhere to fill our hearts, minds, and souls except right at the spiritual being that created us. Some might think we were created in a scientific, evolutionary fashion.

My husband is a "detail" person; I am not. He has read and studied many different theories on how the world and mankind were created, as have many other people I know. His pursuit in understanding different scientific theories is meaningful for him. It is important that he persist to find answers to the questions he has. Conversely, it is simple for me, regardless of how He did it, we are created by God. My questions lie elsewhere.

God created each of us unique, talented and skilled; each having different purposes and different needs. I'm not a person that needs to have all that figured out, but if you are, God would love having conversations about that with you! A word of caution here though, don't let your desires of knowing all the answers become a point of pride or entitlement that keeps you from "knowing" God. Many have shared they won't believe until they have all their questions answered. Their pursuit of knowledge becomes a hindrance to faith. It will be impossible to know everything as we don't have the mind of God.

God isn't scared of your questions; He's not concerned that you will find a scared little wizard behind the curtain like Dorothy did in the Land of Oz. Nothing is too silly, too small, or too big to bring to God in prayer. He may act in ways we cannot understand, believe, or expect but that doesn't mean He isn't listening.

He is the Lord Almighty, creator of heaven and earth (Revelation 1:8, Nehemiah 9:6). He loves His time with you. If you don't see Him in your life, active and loving,

Pride

then I really hope you begin just simply asking Him to "show Himself" in your life. Seeing God often begins with *intentional looking with expectations of seeing*. This requires an open, investigative mind that is not self-centered.

At the end of the day, God wants us to make a choice. God does give us free will. He wants us to be free, not chained to our own prideful jail cells. It's exhausting to be only concerned with trying to fill all our own needs and wants. Are we asking for the things we think we deserve or need, without gratefulness to the One that provides it all?

Many people believe if they work hard and have earned what they have, then what they have is theirs, not something given by God. I did, too. Working hard is something I grew up believing in and still do. Hard work is only part of the equation. Many believe it is their hard work that paves the way into Heaven. Being good enough, or doing enough good deeds, keeps us focused on our own efforts. Self-reliance can be a form of pride. It keeps us from recognizing and being grateful for what God gives us. As Christians, we are ensured a place in heaven not because of what we have done, but because of what God has done. God asks us to act a certain way because of our recognition of what He has done and because of our love for Him (John 14:15, Isaiah 46:9). This is grace. Thinking we have "earned" everything we have is a refusal to see the grace in our lives.

CHAPTER 3

GOD'S ECONOMY

"We make a living by what we get. We make a life by what we give."
—Winston Churchill

"There's a really good chance that I've confused what I 'need' with what I 'want.' And if that's the case, I'm looking for both in the wrong place."
—Craig D. Lounsbrough

Early in our marriage Dave and I would take turns taking care of the finances. He'd do it for some months, and then I would take my turn. It was during my turn that I quickly got us into financial trouble. It got so bad that our savings was depleted, tithing ceased, and I used credit cards to buy groceries and pay the necessary bills that would help me hide the situation from him.

When I brought the truth of our financial mess to Dave, two things happened over two decades ago that have affected me to this day. The first was my husband's reaction. Yes, he was disappointed. He had lived his life devoted to doing the right thing, and that meant paying your debts and giving God what is His. But instead of berating me, yelling, or even reminding me what a mess I'd made, he simply said, "We need to fix this." My husband is all about plans and about what is right, whether someone is paying attention or not.

The second was that God was at work in this situation.

We had recently gone through a financial planning series through our church. That helped us manage in spite of our different personalities. Relieved that my husband wasn't going to make me suffer, I had the courage to tell him that date night was out, there would be no entertainment or fun stuff, and maybe we'd eat beans for the rest of our lives! He laughed and said that wasn't realistic and together we worked on our budget.

First, Dave was paying our tithe and not just the ten percent for the current paycheck, but for the entire back tithe that was not paid. Then we would take a certain amount of cash and put it in envelopes for me to use for groceries, necessities, and entertainment. We would pay our necessary bills, mortgage, electric, water, minimums on everything else and work extra on the smallest debt that we could pay off the easiest. Once one of those debts was paid off, we would begin to work on the next one until, eventually, we were debt free.

On paper, we were in the red for quite a while. I committed to carrying a small notebook to log every purchase before entering a store. I stopped wandering the aisles, and I told myself many times, "You don't need this." Soon I discovered that I didn't. It was a time of intentional persistence and a time of incredible suffering and deprivation. But, in the midst of all that, God showed up in an incredible way.

Seeing our budget on paper and the time it would take to pay it off was overwhelming. It seemed too big. We prayed together, dedicated our finances to God, and committed to paying the entire tithe we owed, first. This was the scary part for me because we didn't have the money. However, my husband was resolute. There was no negotiation regarding this issue.

So we prayed.

Dave decided to sell some of our stock. That would take care of some of the tithe, but it would take away from our long-term investments and retirement. After we made that decision, just before we transferred the stock to the church the shares jumped in value to cover almost all of our unpaid tithes. Dave used to write patents while in law school and soon after this he got a call to ask if he could pick up some extra work. To this day, I remember that Dave had to work overtime at his day job and then come home to work many more hours to pay for my selfishness. He never, not once, complained or blamed or resented me.

I began to watch my nephew as a way to earn extra money. This became a blessing because he became our surrogate son as we had three daughters. I often joke that his mom has to share.

After Dave came home from work, and on weekends, I worked as a bartender and waitress. It was hard, it was difficult, it required persistence, and it was a time when we had to exhibit self-control in every financial decision. I had no credit cards and no debit cards. I only dealt in cash, and I can truly say it was as freeing as it was difficult. It got easier to tell myself I didn't need things and coming clean about what I spent lifted a load off my back. My husband was generous with his love for me but did not enable me to put us in that position ever again.

I am confident in saying that the stock prices doubling or tripling, whatever it was, in the days immediately before we sold was God multiplying what we gave Him. The extra work, my husband's attitude, and the debts that were taken care of were all part of the huge and incredible blessing I received during that time. I believe that within three months, what didn't work out on paper for more than triple that time became a reality and we were in the black. Just by a little, but we were back on track.

> *"Give generously to them and do so without a grudging heart; then because of this the Lord your God will bless you in all your work and in everything you put your hand to"* (Deuteronomy 15:10).

I had put us into debt, but Dave was generous with his love, mercy, wisdom, diligence, and discipline. During a very difficult time, he gave everything he had to help us accomplish what was right and what God asked us to do. He did it without resentment and not once did he mention the steep price he was paying for what I had done. God blessed the work Dave put his hands to and used his heart to allow me to see and experience love in a way I never had before.

> "Speaking to the church at Corinth, Paul said "you will be enriched in every way so that you can be generous on every occasion, and through us your generosity will result in thanksgiving to God" (2 Corinthians 9:11).

I remember that time and also remember how my husband's generosity mirrored how generous God had been with us. I have never withheld our tithe again and often pray for opportunities to give more as God leads us. Being generous never cost us anything we needed. God has always paid his own way. In fact, He's never asked us to give something He didn't give us. I've learned that if I want to be generous, then I have to stop saying, "I need, I want" and start asking, "God what do they need, what do You want?" That's when I've seen over and over that true generosity happens when God begins to multiply the things we give. In reality, what we have to give, in comparison to what God has and what He has given to us, is really quite small.

> "Bring all the tithes into the storehouse so there will be enough food in my Temple. If you do," says the Lord of Heaven's Armies, "I will open the windows of heaven for you. I will pour out a blessing so great you won't have enough room to take it in! Try it! Put me to the test!" (Malachi 3:10).

This verse is one that Dave knew and was committed to acting upon early in our marriage. He trusted God and acted in faith, not just words. He knew that what God promises, He accomplishes. It looks different for everyone and in each situation, but God did open the floodgates when my heart was in the right place. I stopped stealing from Him and deceiving my husband. We took a leap of faith and made a deposit into his storehouse. God can make do without what I can give Him, but Dave and I know we cannot make do without what God gives us.

In Luke 12, Jesus teaches the disciples to not worry, and he starts off with this advice: *"Therefore I tell you, do not worry about your life, what you will eat; or about your body, what you will wear. For life is more than food, and the body more than clothes."*

Jesus is telling them that there is more to life than our own needs. Jesus even asks them, *"How can worrying add a single hour to your life?"* Jesus sets the stage on how God dresses and clothes the earth, He created, and then Jesus urges his listeners in verse 29, *"Do not set your heart on what you will eat or drink; do not worry about it . . ."* but rather (in verse 31) *"seek his kingdom, and these things will be given to you as well."*

Jesus knows that we will be focused on our needs. We will also be tempted to be self-serving—feeding our pride and satisfying our own desires. Knowing this, Jesus tells us that God is concerned with more than just giving us what we need. Life adds up to more than the sum of our needs when He is involved. God isn't saying don't bring your needs to him; He's saying that life is more than these needs and He is concerned about it all. He wants to give us MORE than we can hold, touch, consume or imagine. But if your heart and mind are focused on your needs more than they are focused on what God wants to give you, you will miss out on a richer life.

I understand that saying this to the homeless and people who are barely surviving is not helpful. Survival is a serious issue and meeting basic needs are absolutely essential. I have not mentioned these verses lightheartedly and nonchalantly. I have starved and gone without meals and walked hours to get to an interview at McDonald's. I have stolen things because I was poor, but felt entitled. I have used a grocery cart to take my things home because I didn't have a car to carry them.

Imagine that from a generous heart, after we've been blessed with things, that we, in turn, bless others. Just think that once we know someone has a need, that we do everything in our power to help them. What if, during our prayer time, we ask to be a blessing to others?

I'm advocating for people to choose to help and for all to look out for others. I was poor for many reasons, most of which I caused myself because of bad decisions. I was looking for something more, but the places I looked to satisfy this "more" were just temporary. Those pursuits were hurting me. They were just temporary fixes, whether from food, alcohol, short-term relationships, caring too much about the opinion and approval of others, or desiring material possessions. In the end, it was never enough, and I fell back into a very self-defeating spiral.

Ask any drug addict, alcoholic, overeater, or any other slave to an addiction trying to fill a void only God can reach. Some addictions look healthier than others. Being fit, good looking, or wanting to work hard isn't bad; it's only when these needs take the place of God that it becomes a problem.

Jesus ends the lesson (in Luke 12, on not worrying) by telling the disciples (verses 33-34):

> *". . . provide purses for yourselves that will not wear out, a treasure in heaven that will never fail, where no thief comes near and no moth destroys. For where your treasure is, there your heart will be also."*

CHAPTER 4

OUR HEARTS AND MOTIVES

"I give you my hand, I give you my love more precious than money, I give you myself before preaching or law; will you give me yourself?"
—Walt Whitman

"Don't Gain the World and Lose Your Soul, Wisdom Is Better Than Silver or Gold."
—Bob Marley

With our hearts, it's a two-way street. We let things in, and we let things out. God wants us to protect our heart, to be careful what we let in and then to guard the treasure He has placed in our heart. In Proverbs 4:23, we are advised: *"Above all else, guard your heart, for everything you do flows from it."* God wants to give us things we value and will use in a way that show we understand their value.

Haven't most of us felt that doubt of giving something to someone who we thought wouldn't value what we gave them? What about that person who looks so desperate, but we hesitate to give because we are sure they'll use that money to buy drugs or alcohol instead of food? I used to think of these things primarily because I was that person. I spent my money on things that weren't good for me. My husband, while he was in college, would see people in need, but instead of giving them money, he gave them food. He'd buy them a meal and give it to them. How much is that like God, wanting to give us what we REALLY need and will value, instead of giving us what we can use to hurt ourselves? It may not be what we are asking for, but it's what we need. My husband did not want to be an enabler, and neither does God. That means, if we don't give room to the thought that He knows better what is good for us and what we REALLY need, our pride will get in the way.

Sometimes we don't get the things we so desperately want yet shouldn't have. God uses everything to His good purpose (Philippians 2:13), so we know that when we are focused on what He would like us to focus on, things will work out. If we make a mistake and earnestly turn to Him, He earnestly turns to us. For me, I am eternally grateful that He is patient and compassionate (Psalm 145:8) and that He is concerned with my heart so that when I make poor decisions or ask for things with wrong motives or ask for things that will hurt me, He will not enable me.

God gives us choices, always. He is concerned with how we feel and why we do things. References to the word "heart," whether it's ours or His, are made over five hundred times in the Bible.[1] There is another important aspect of prayer which is important in God's economy—your motive and the condition of your heart. In James 4:2-3:

> *"You do not have because you do not ask God. When you ask, you do not receive, because you ask with wrong motives, that you may spend what you get on your pleasures."*

In regard to our prayer lives, this brings up many questions: Are our motives in alignment with His will? Are we being selfish? Is this something God wants to give us? If not, what does He want us to have?

Selfishness is defined as being concerned chiefly with one's own personal profit or pleasure.[2] To spend or use what God gives us solely for our own pleasure is part of having the wrong motives. God is not interested in giving us things so we become indulgent, entitled, and self-seeking. All of that would be in opposition to what He does want for us, which is to look for something bigger and better than ourselves. So, when we pray, asking for something solely for our own gain would be futile.

Mankind is generally selfish; we are born that way. If you don't believe me, spend a day or two with any baby, toddler, or small child. Most will do what they are able to satisfy their desires. They can be self-centered, looking for ways to make themselves noticed or heard. They aren't evil or malicious; they just have a very small world at which they are the center. God wants our world to be bigger than anything that we can imagine so that it will include Him and prayer is a part of that. Meditation or repetition of scripture is a great way of "praying through scripture." One that I use frequently and can be helpful in revealing the motives of our hearts is Psalm 139:23-24:

"Search me, O God, and know my heart; Try me and know my anxious thoughts; And see if there be any hurtful way in me; And lead me in the everlasting way."

By meditating on a specific verse, we can train our mind to invite God in. This verse, in particular, invites God into our hearts so that things can come to our minds that we need to examine in our lives, whether it's our attitude, lack of humility, pride, anger, or whatever issues God would like us to deal with.

God is concerned with our hearts. If they are "obstinate, cold, and hard," entities lacking in tenderness they are like stones, unchanging and unreachable.[3] Hearts of stone are not suitable for the residence of the Holy Spirit. Just as God cannot be found by a person who will not open their mind, the Holy Spirit cannot be contained in a rigid heart. The Holy Spirit is given to us by God for our benefit, and our hearts will change if we allow God to make that very valuable deposit:

> *"A new heart also will I give you, and a new spirit will I put within you: and I will take away the stony heart out of your flesh, and I will give you a heart of flesh"* (Ezekiel 36:26).

This verse references both a new heart and a new spirit that God will put in us. Stones are heavy, solid, unmoving, and empty of life. Charles Spurgeon makes several comments on this topic in his sermon "The Stony Heart Removed."[4] He first talks about the "Stony heart and its dangers" and gives us a picture of a stony heart: "cold, dead, and hard." His description tells us that this heart is not easily softened and is incapable of receiving impressions. He is not referring to a physical heart but a heart that cannot be used by God—"a heart impervious to all instrumentality." Why is this important to God? Simply put, God wants a relationship with us, but we cannot have one with Him if we are primarily concerned with ourselves and our own well-being, refusing to notice, acknowledge, or be influenced by Him. Relationships are made of connections, one thing influencing another. Relationships are founded on the premise of separate entities affecting one other. How hard would that be if one person didn't acknowledge the other?

A "heart of flesh" signifies life, vitality, flexibility, growth, softness, and vulnerability. In the second part of his sermon, Spurgeon describes a heart of flesh in this way:

"What is meant by a "heart of flesh?" It means a heart that can feel on account of sin—a heart that can bleed when the arrows of God stick fast in it; it means a heart that can yield when the gospel makes its attacks—a heart that can be impressed when the seal of God's word comes upon it; it means a heart that is warm, for life is warm—a heart that can think, a heart that can aspire, a heart that can love—putting all in one—a heart of flesh means that new heart and right spirit which God giveth to the regenerate. But wherein does this heart of flesh consist; wherein does its tenderness consist? Well, its tenderness consists in three things. There is a tenderness of conscience. Men who have lost their stony hearts are afraid of sin; even before sin they are afraid of it."[5]

This may be a little formal, but it is elegantly said. "A heart that is warm, for life is warm, a heart that can think, a heart that can aspire, a heart that can love . . . a tenderness of conscience." This is a heart that God can place His treasure in, and this is a heart worth guarding (2 Timothy 1:14). In God's economy, our hearts are so very valuable. He wants them to be open so He can make the deposits of his currency. *"This is the confidence we have in approaching God: that if we ask anything according to his will, He hears us"* (1 John 5:14).

So what does God want to give us? Power? Money? Fame? Fortune? He can, but His economy is not the same as ours. Power does not mean relentlessly and ruthlessly acquiring and conquering things and people. Being rich and prospering doesn't always mean financially and materialistically. In fact, scripture talks about what God does want to give us, and it's something we cannot take or buy from another to use for ourselves. It is intangible and priceless . . . something called peace. In Philippians 4:6-7, it says that peace is something He wants to give us:

> *"Be anxious for nothing, but in everything, by prayer and petition, with thanksgiving, present your requests to God. And the peace of God, which surpasses all understanding, will guard your hearts and your minds in Christ Jesus."*

How many times do we pray for money or something tangible when we really need peace? Anybody can rip a dollar bill out of a hand, but not many can remove peace from a heart that God has enshrined in love. In terms of being confident that God hears our hearts and our prayers, knowing what He wants for us is vital. He knows peace is a priceless commodity. That doesn't mean He won't give you money, but it means God wants to give you peace "in everything," and when we come to Him, God promises to give that to us. He also promises so much more.

His economy deals in love, mercy, compassion, hope, wisdom, forgiveness, and freedom. He has plans that we prosper (Deuteronomy 29:9, Jeremiah 29:11) and that our lives will always be lived with Him (Psalm 27:4). When we face our darkest days, He wants to comfort us, deliver us from our troubles, and give us good things (Psalm 23:4). He wants to work everything for good and to provide for all our needs (Romans 8:28, Philippians 4:19). He wants to give us an advocate that never leaves us, and wants to love us for eternity (John 14:16, Romans 8:38-39).

This is just a sampling of the things God finds valuable and wants to give us. Many of them are conditional, because He wants us to choose Him, rely on Him, trust in Him, and have a relationship with Him. All are things we cannot buy: peace, comfort, a place of refuge, knowledge, being loved, being filled with His helper (the Holy Spirit), having our paths made straight, and forgiveness. He wants us to know that He loves us fully, completely, and unfailingly. We have an eternal home with Him in heaven when we choose Him. He has a plan for us, and each one of us is special and created by Him. God is a supernatural being, and as such, we are given strength by our faith in Him. These are far different things from what a materialistic economy is based upon, but God is not in the business of portfolios as much as He is in the business of reconciling our hearts to Him so that we can be with Him for eternity. His deposits are not made into a metal safe, locked by a combination so that few may gain access; His deposits are made into every heart that calls on Him. His deposits are meant to be shared with everyone. God's economy is eternal and communal. He wants us to help each other and look to Him. In Matthew 18:18-20 (*The Message*), Jesus says:

> "What you say to one another is eternal, I mean this. When two of you get together on anything at all on earth and make a prayer of it, my Father in heaven goes into action. And when two or three of you are together because of me, you can be sure that I'll be there."

Since God's economy promises us many good things and deals with personal deposits placed in our hearts, it makes sense that our motives are extremely important to Him. Isn't that the same with us? When we give someone something, don't we want to give more to someone who values what was given? God is love, and God is good; He doesn't give things to us to harm us or harm others. How much more impactful could our prayers be if we asked with motives driven by love and goodness instead of things that only make us more selfish and more self-focused?

We can't hide our hearts from God. In Ecclesiastes 11:9, it says we can *"follow the ways of our hearts and whatever our eyes see, but know that for all these things God will bring us into judgment."* God is concerned with what our heart's desire and where we look to gather our treasure as well as where we look to spend our blessings. Are we asking God for blessings while bitterness, lack of forgivingness, selfishness, anger, or anything else takes up all the room in our hearts so that there isn't room for God to make His divine deposit? He won't give us things that are meant to be used in a manner that contradicts His character. He is so many things, but He is not evil. Praying in a manner that is intent on nurturing a heart filled with vengefulness, bitterness, lack of forgivingness, or harm for others is counterproductive. If we choose all of those things on our own, then we will be judged by Him and called to account for our motives and actions. John Bevere, in his book *The Bait of Satan*, writes that "only God has the right to judge . . . we must not take the prerogatives of God into our own hands. It is wrong to do a right thing in the wrong way."[6] Although our motives are vital, that doesn't give anyone a free pass to do anything they want "for the right reasons." Our actions are still a part of our accounting that God will call us to.

In addition to an economy that is vastly different than the one we typically focus on, God also has things to say about hidden treasure. In Isaiah 45:3, God promises to *"give treasures hidden in the darkness—secret riches. I will do this so you may know that I am the LORD, the God of Israel, the one who calls you by name."* The message in Isaiah is two-fold; there is a promise and a reason. There are treasures

He wants to give us, and He tells us why He will give them to us. His purpose is not solely, nor primarily, to make us happy, but He gives so that we *"will know He is the Lord, the God of Israel."* This isn't a statement from a prideful God, an egomaniac who wants only our servitude and rule following. This statement is one that calls for reverence, awe, trust, and intimacy. Anyone who has been in awe of the majesty of a sunset or the enormity of the ocean has only experienced a hint of the glory of God. That sunset isn't prideful or an egomaniac, it just simply "is." That's how God's glory is; He just simply "is." He wants us to recognize who He is first so that we can then begin to trust that He can do what He says He can do.

The last part of that verse says, *"the one who calls you by name."* This is a statement of intimacy at an individual level. He gives to us so that we can respond to Him on a personal level. Learning about God and praying for His revelations in our hearts and minds helps simple faith grow. Our faith grows by asking questions and learning how God wants us to affect the world around us. In context, this verse was taken from a chapter written about Cyrus the Great, King of Persia (Isaiah 45:1-7).

King Cyrus was not an Israelite, but God called him by name and by doing so, God acknowledged him in a very personal and individual way. God *"strengthens him, supports him, and helps him take down other kings."* He promises *"to go before him and level the mountains and break down gates of bronze and cut through bars of iron."* This king had not yet acknowledged that God is Lord over all but God promised him hidden treasures.

In verse 13, Isaiah wrote that God would *"raise up Cyrus in His righteousness and He will make all his ways straight."*

The historic figure, King Cyrus, would rebuild God's city and set His exiles free. The book of Isaiah was written about one hundred and sixty years before King Cyrus even ruled and about one hundred years before the city was destroyed.[8]

God has been working for our benefit and according to His plans far longer than we can imagine. Some things don't change, because God's purpose and love for us is unchanging (Hebrews 6:17). He keeps all His promises, and His word is true (Psalm 89:34). How He describes Himself in the Bible does not change for governments or for the politically correct or for any whim of a particular society or culture (James 1:17). Who He is for one, He is for all. For everyone who *"asks, seeks, and knocks,"* He will be found. We can ask God through prayer what this verse means for us today and for us as individuals. Through our prayer lives, when we sit with God and ask Him about His truths, He will reveal Himself and His truths because that is what He does. For those who look and pursue Him, He wants to be found. His purpose hasn't changed since the beginning of time, and that includes a relationship with us. Are we thinking the same way as God or are we only concerned with our own needs and our own comforts? As we get to know who God is and what He wants for us, we can transform our thoughts and, through prayer, transform our lives.

The treasure spoken of in Isaiah is abundant, but it is hidden in obscurity, in a secret place, in a place of protection. In King Cyrus' time, this hidden treasure may have been literal, hidden treasure of another king. It is logical to have a storehouse for our treasures that cannot be ransacked or stolen; we protect the things we are attached to, the things we value and love. That's why we lock our doors at night before we go to bed and are not on watch. In this verse, God will be giving treasures to Cyrus—*"the treasures hidden in the darkness."* He will be giving Cyrus secret riches.

Why was this recorded? Why does God want us to know that He gave something to Cyrus that belonged to another even before it happened? In the literal sense and in respect to our prayer lives, God has the power to take and give whatever He pleases. No one can hold onto something He does not want them to have, and no one can keep something from us that He wants to give us, no matter how well it is hidden. Everything is His, not ours; and this will be true from the beginning of time to the end of it. As we pray for the things we would like to have, are we praying so that we will be an instrument in His cause? He moves resources from one hand to another to make that happen.

In the New Testament, Jesus taught difficult spiritual truths through stories and parables. Not everyone understood what Jesus taught (Matthew 13:13), but for those who sought truth, He wanted it to be clear. He would have used situations and examples that would have been culturally understood and very clear to those listening and seeking truth. The stories would have made it easier to make the connection to the spiritual truth Jesus wanted to teach.[9]

In addition to its historical fact, the verse in Isaiah can be a parable of sorts for an invaluable truth for our prayer lives and for our pursuit of God. That truth is that He has hidden things so that He can reveal them to us. He protects valuable treasure so that when we pursue His truth, we find what we are looking for.

> *"For there is nothing hidden, except that it should be made known, neither was anything made secret, but that it should be found"* (Mark 4:22).

> *"There is nothing concealed that will not be disclosed, or hidden that will not be made known. What you have said in the dark will be heard in the daylight, and what you have whispered in the ear in the inner rooms will be proclaimed from the roofs"* (Luke 12:2-3).

As children, many of us have played the game of "hide and seek." There are many variations of it, and the game is played throughout the world. In Spain, the game is called "el escondite," in France, "jeu de cache-cache," in Israel, "machboim," in South Korea, "sumbaggoggil," and in Romania, "de-av-atiascunselea."[10] It's in our nature to want to find something valuable that is hidden. God wired us this way, and He hides things so that we can find them. For many of us, it is through our search, our struggle, our work, that we find His treasure more valuable than anything else here on earth. In our prayer lives, we can ask God to make the connections for us that are written in the Bible regardless of the historical context of when they were written. Although the Bible is made up of different books with different intentions and themes which transcend different cultures and were written by different authors, through prayer it becomes personal and conversational. God can speak directly to us through His word. We can find layers of meanings that make the Bible more personal and intimate for our lives.

CHAPTER 5

WHY PRAY? PIVOTAL EVENT

"Change how you see and see how you change."
—Zen proverb

"It gives me a deep comforting sense that things seen are temporal and things unseen are eternal."
—Helen Keller

My journey with God and in prayer has led me to many wonderful and impactful experiences and revelations. These three observations are what I have found the most important:

- Prayers are not about being perfect, but rather they are about relationship. Start where you are and be persistent.
- Pride is the great stumbling block to our prayers. Pride elevates us above God. We need to know who He is before we can trust Him with our hearts.
- God has His own economy. He is relational. He has made promises of what He wants to give us and is concerned with the motives of our hearts.

COME FILL THIS PLACE

The Bible tells us to pray persistently and in everything (Luke 18:1), and that would be a wonderful goal to strive for. There are moments in everyone's life that bring a change in perspective. Those moments herald a new way of existing, so much so that you can't go back to the way it was.

There was such a time in my life that affected my prayers. It gave new meaning to the term "prayer life." I learned that prayers, each one of them, are vital and have meaning in the spiritual world and are more meaningful and impactful than we know. Although I don't fully comprehend all the details of the term "prayer life," what I experienced changed my prayers and gave them "life." It helped me understand, just a little more, why we need to pray persistently and in everything we do.

Our prayers matter, just like our hearts and souls matter to God. Having a relationship with God, sharing what we have in our hearts, and then looking for His involvement in our lives and listening to what He tells us gives our prayers life. With Him, they grow, evolve, and affect our own lives and the lives of others in ways we cannot imagine.

Years ago, I traveled to Russia with a group of strangers. Our team was assembled from all over the United States, and none of us had ever met. We all knew the leader, but not one another. There were many friends, church groups, and other believers in the states who had been praying for the success of this mission trip.

Traveling into unknown territory was very unnerving to me. I'm a cowardly homebody who gets lost going around the block. I also have abandonment issues, so traveling to another country without my husband and with strangers was just one reason I started praying earnestly for God's provision. As time got closer to boarding our individual flights, things started happening to hinder our travels. Injuries, complications, and just plain weirdness ensued. Most of us saw it as spiritual warfare, evil spiritual forces that oppose God and the good He wants us to do. I developed a very embarrassing and huge boil, overnight, that would make sitting on a plane for all those hours extremely painful. This was something I had never experienced before and haven't since. Without time to see a doctor to have it lanced and treated, we treated it at home, and my husband and I prayed that none of us would be stopped from boarding our flights. To this day, I am amazed at what many of the women had to overcome to get to their flights: concussions, extreme knee pain, back pain, etc.

Each lady on the team had a job to do. We were brought there to co-facilitate a group of ladies through a post-abortion study that helps women heal from those procedures. I had made many bad decisions in life and had benefited greatly from this study (even though I was sure I didn't need it before going through it). I had spent years trying to help women heal from their choice to abort by helping them walk through the steps of this study. When doing this study in the States, we would plan on 6-12 weeks or more, depending on the timeframe and scheduling.

It's complicated to unravel thoughts, feelings, and issues people are unable to deal with when they don't think they need help. In Russia, my co-facilitator and I had three days to lead our small group of women through this study. My concern was trying to do this with a translator and in such a short time. Doing it when everyone spoke English was complicated enough.

As we had been praying for God to be seen and heard for months before we even got on our flights, though amazed, I was not surprised that God was seen and heard. A stranger from an entirely different part of the United States, who served as my partner in leading these women through the study, was an answer to prayer, as were both our translators. Things that we didn't know to ask for when we prayed for our ideal translators were given to us. One example was that my co-facilitator preferred to think of the sentences she wanted to say, stop, and then allow her translator to translate. She could pick up on her train of thought and continue with her next few sentences, allow for the translation, and repeat this process until she completed her thoughts. I would never have functioned this way because of how I think. Stopping and waiting would have been too distracting for me. The translator assigned to me was just what I needed. I lowered my voice and spoke quietly, and she translated to the ladies while I was speaking, reflecting my intonations and tone perfectly. She literally became my voice so I could continue speaking and not get distracted. I didn't even know until we started our group that translators could have that kind of impact and still thank God that He had us covered on things we knew nothing about and didn't even know to ask for.

We were able to take these ladies through this study in three days, in a foreign language and in multiple layers that are usually taught separately. We addressed their own hurts and needs and helped teach them how to bring others through the same study and to do it safely, as they were trying to reach women in an atmosphere that does not embrace Christianity. It was truly amazing how much they absorbed and learned and how God communicated for us despite language and cultural differences . . . but this was only the beginning.

Up to this point, my prayers mostly consisted of the things that were needed physically, materialistically, and spiritually. I also prayed for others and what they needed, but truthfully I did not spend much time in prayer other than to kind of "toss up" my list of desires to God. It wasn't about spending time with Him, it wasn't continual, and it wasn't a whole lot of recognizing who He is and considering that. It wasn't a time to spend getting to know Him, as it was mostly about me and sometimes about others. The next few days would change my perspective. I can't write about all the ways He showed Himself to me on that trip, but I will share the most impactful . . . and the most unexplainable.

At one point, we did a prayer exercise with just our team. I had not done this exercise before. The more experienced leaders took the less experienced through so we could see what it looked like. We each had different jobs; ladies who were experienced in intercessory prayer were first in line.

Intercessory prayer is praying for someone else and on their behalf even when they are not able or willing to do so.[1] Galatians 6:2 tells us that we should *"Carry each other's burdens, and in this way, you will fulfill the law of Christ."* This type of prayer can also be referred to as "standing in the gap." Sin separates us from God, creating a division; a gap. Man's fall from the Garden of Eden formed a gap. We can "stand in" for someone else—just as Jesus did for us, with our prayers. If a person prays for another who is going through difficulty or trouble, then those prayers are intercessory in nature. Another aspect of this kind of prayer is when reconciliation is being petitioned for. Often prayers for loved ones and friends who don't know God, are intercessory as well. These intercessory prayers for reconciliation are often pleading for salvation for a loved one or friend who is lost.

I knew very little about this.

In the exercise, one of our team members took one of two seats in the middle, and we sat in a semicircle around those two chairs. We would be praying for her as someone led her through some questions that she would respond to. The rest of us did not participate in any way, except through prayer. We didn't even have to listen to what was being said.

I was sitting close to a door that was slightly ajar and had stretched out my leg so that it was in the open doorway. Within a few minutes, my leg felt like it was on fire, like it was physically burning. It was so real that I thought I could smell the burning flesh. I realized it was spiritual because I did open my eyes and look at my leg to confirm there were no flames! Prior to this moment, I had never experienced this and didn't know what to do. Just one thought came to my mind, and through the pain I felt, I repeated it over and over: "I will not move my leg. I will not move my leg." Saying those words meant something important, that I would stand right there where God had placed me for that moment. My fight was to keep that door from closing, that somehow if I refused to move no matter how intense the pain, I could keep that door open. I found out later that, spiritually speaking, that open door was the ministry of the woman in the center and that she was at a crossroad on whether she would continue on God's behalf.

What she shared with us later was that she had been wounded terribly and had thought she had forgiven her offender. She realized during that exercise that she was at a fork in the road because God had been asking her to pray for her attacker's salvation and she did not want to do that. She knew that her ministry would become compromised by her bitterness, anger, and lack of forgiveness. While Satan was reminding her of every offense she had experienced and every reason she had to hold on to her rage, my leg burned. We all (unknowingly) prayed, and we all stood our ground on her behalf when she couldn't. This was a spiritual battle. God wanted prayers for a condemned man because He wants even the worst of us to give Him our hearts. What God gives freely to one, He gives to all.

As she was fighting this battle in her mind and heart, I felt the burning pain and smelled that horrible smell. Still, something filled me. It was a mixture of softness as well as resolve or strength. I didn't know what to call it. I begged, pleaded, worshipped, and cried inside for her, a lady I hardly knew, and continued to stand (or sit) right where I was, too stubborn to move my leg.

At some point, a light broke through the winter clouds in the window of the other room that the door led to. It shone brighter and brighter until it reached my leg and I knew I could stop praying. I felt peace, overwhelming warmth and love. The pain, with its burning sensation along with the sense of evil, was gone. Instead, a bright, soft but intense light took its place. As we talked later, we heard her story, and I knew that I had experienced a spiritual battle. I understood a little more about what an intercessor does.

Another aspect of standing in the gap for another can be shown through the examples of the soldiers that hunker down in gaps when they are trying to avoid gunfire while trying to hold their ground in battle. We can hunker down in "the gap" of someone else's battle. We are protected to some degree, because it is not our spiritual battle, but theirs. This is a spiritual gap because the ones who are praying are not being attacked and are protected by separation from the enemy. Although I have never been in a real military battle, this visual helps me understand a Biblical principle about standing in the gap for others. It's not me facing the spiritual battle, so I can stand in the gap for another and pray with undivided attention and focus. While they are facing their spiritual battle and real-life attacks, we in the gap are unaffected while praying for their protection and provision. What she shared later broke our hearts in happiness. She told us she would pray for the offender before we even asked. In my eyes, she was doing something extraordinary. Her heart was now in line with God's will. The brightness on her face showed how her heart came out of that battle with God by her side. Through prayer, God uses the most broken parts of us to do what we can't imagine ever doing. Through Him, we do what is "extra" ordinary and, in that, we reflect His own character.

The next day as we did the same exercise we split up into smaller groups. I was standing behind the girl from Russia that I was interceding for, and I was not to be involved in any way while she was going through her exercise. As I stood behind her and prayed with my eyes closed, a very real evil shot straight through my bones. As indescribable as it was, I was terrified, but because of the experience the day prior, I now knew what to call it. I prayed through my terror. I felt as though if I turned around I would see hell right behind me. This sounds dramatic, but for anyone who experiences this kind of warfare, it can be quite immobilizing.

As she sat calmly in her chair, quietly, with tears running down her face, a fierce spiritual battle was going on for her soul. We can't see all that is going on, but God loves us fiercely, and He fights for us to be with Him. Spiritual battles are not pretty; Satan is evil and wants no part of God's plan for us. Without our knowledge, in the moments while she quietly wept, my Russian friend was making an eternal decision. As she was doing this and as I was praying quietly for her, I experienced what I call a glimmer into a spiritual world that I could no longer deny. It was terrifying and by far the most frightening thing that I have experienced to date. Yet, as I stood my ground in the dry, burnt wooded area, refusing to give into the darkness behind me, I saw a light moving toward me. There are no words that could adequately describe it, but it felt like love, peace, comfort, and security all rolled into one soft, luminous light. It felt immense, and, although brilliant, it had a soft glow. It moved forward, slowly filling the space in front of me. I knew in my heart something significant had happened in my Russian friend's life. As the light filled the space before me and the darkness fell away behind me, I was greatly relieved. We learned later after talking with her that she had decided to give her life to God, and as a result of that experience, I am bonded to her forever.

In another instance, I saw a spirit of fear leave one of the Russian women. Fear crippled her life and even showed on her face. I literally saw something leave her body as I crouched behind the closest woman from our team who was calling all of us to pray for this girl as she lay on the ground shaking. I was scared out of my mind, having never seen or experienced this kind of thing. Again, I fought the urge to run; even covering my mouth and nose in case whatever was causing this girl to convulse would come out and enter my body. I don't know why at the time I thought my hand would be a good defense against what I saw. Meanwhile, while crouching behind my friend, timidly hiding behind her boldness, I learned (like in any battle) in the field by her example. She was brave because of who God is and because of what Jesus did for us, and she was confident through her faith (not in herself) that she would be able to stand by this girl who clearly had something happening to her. As we prayed and others gathered around, something left her. I can't explain it. It resembled a gray, dark shadow of sorts, and it freaked me out. What came after was truly amazing. The girl sat up, and her face had changed; the fear we could clearly see on her face earlier was gone. Gone. I even wanted to take a picture of her because I couldn't believe it could be that obvious. She said, in her own words, that she was free from the fear that had consumed her throughout her life. I'll never forget the freedom that shone from her pretty blue eyes.

These are just a few accounts of what happened during that trip. After what was experienced in Russia, my prayers changed. I can't pray the way I used to, and I never will. Others might think its make-believe because they can't touch it. Others might want some kind of scientific explanation for what I experienced. Physically I'm unable to show you what transpired or take you to the places I saw. I can't pass on the emotions and thoughts I experienced to another heart and mind. Like most things, someone who reads these words will have to decide for themselves if what I'm writing will have an impact on their life. For me, I choose to believe that God blessed me with a peek into the spiritual warfare that He's talking about in Ephesians 6, and it's more real to me than anything I will see this side of heaven.

A journey in faith can be as unique as the individual who walks that road, but one constant is that a choice will ultimately have to be made, to follow or not to follow. It takes a moment to make that choice, but it's a decision that begins a journey that lasts not just for this lifetime, but for eternity. Our choices have both physical and spiritual repercussions. I was privileged to get a small glimpse of how our prayers have value in the spiritual world on that short trip.

Each one of us will be fought for, will be sought after, and will be waited for. I believe this with all my heart. He wants the damaged, the unwanted, and the undeserving along with every other soul that walks, has walked, and will ever walk this earth. There was a reason that on the cross, with criminals being crucified on his left and right, that Jesus said, *"Father, forgive them, for they do not know what they are doing"* (Luke 23:34). Even in his pain and sorrow, his heart was filled with love for people who don't know what they are doing. He wasn't just praying for those criminals; he was praying for us all. It was a simple short conversation between Jesus and his Father on our behalf, on behalf of every soul from the beginning of creation to the end.

Our prayers don't need to be complicated or righteous sounding, but they need to be earnest and express, plainly, what is in our hearts. Ultimately, hopefully, our prayer life grows and changes us.

CHAPTER 6

GOD IS SUPERNATURAL— WE'RE NOT!

"Mystery creates wonder and wonder is the basis of man's desire to understand."
—Neil Armstrong

"Any fool can count the seeds in an apple. Only God can count all the apples in one seed."
—Robert H. Schuller

Having a conversation that is focused on the supernatural can be tricky. There are pockets of society that are comfortable with this word, but the idea of a supernatural battle is probably not on the top of the list of subjects to have a cup of coffee over. Regardless of the fact that we may not focus on the supernatural nature of God in our daily lives, His presence is an ever-present reality no matter what condition our lives are in.

When I am speaking of the supernatural things of God, I am talking about things not of this world. I'm speaking to the phenomena that God creates things that cannot be explained by natural laws. To be clear, this is not about magic, witchcraft, or the occult. I'm not talking about people trying to control another's actions in any way, shape, or form. God does not conform to our way of thinking, and He does not behave through what we consider normal human behavior (Isaiah 55:9). Although He created the physical laws of nature, I doubt He is bound by them. He is timeless. His resources are limitless (Jeremiah 32:17).

In the Bible, some of my favorite verses about God's power are in Job chapters 38 and 39. When I'm feeling self-righteous and need to know there are bigger things at work, or when I'm feeling unworthy and need to know who I belong to, reading any part of this gives me an immediate reality check. Here is an excerpt of the scripture where God is describing himself:

> *"Then the Lord spoke to Job out of the storm:*
>
> *He said, "Who is this that obscures my plans with words without knowledge? Brace yourself like a man; I will question you, and you shall answer me.*
>
> *Where were you when I laid the earth's foundation?*
>
> *Tell me, if you understand. Who marked off its dimensions? Surely you know! Who stretched a measuring line across it? On what were its footings set, or who laid its cornerstone while the morning stars sang together and all the angels shouted for joy?*
>
> *Who shut up the sea behind doors when it burst forth from the womb, when I made the clouds its garment and wrapped it in thick darkness, when I fixed limits for it and set its doors and bars in place, when I said, this far you may come and no farther; here is where your proud waves halt.*
>
> *Have you ever given orders to the morning, or shown the dawn its place, that it might take the earth by the edges and shake the wicked out of it?*

> *The earth takes shape like clay under a seal; its features stand out like those of a garment.*
>
> *Have you journeyed to the springs of the sea or walked in the recesses of the deep? Have the gates of death been shown to you?*
>
> *Have you seen the gates of the deepest darkness? Have you comprehended the vast expanses of the Earth?*
>
> *What is the way to the abode of light? And where does darkness reside? Can you take them to their places? Do you know the paths to their dwellings?*
>
> *Have you entered the storehouses of the snow or seen the storehouses of the hail, which I reserve for times of trouble, for days of war and battle?*
>
> *Can you bind the chains of the Pleiades? Can you loosen Orion's belt? Can you bring forth the constellations in their seasons or lead out the Bear with its cubs?*
>
> *Do you know the laws of the heavens? Can you set up God's dominion over the earth? Can you raise your voice to the clouds and cover yourself with a flood of water?*
>
> *Do you send the lightning bolts on their way? Do they report to you, 'Here we are'?"*

All of these verses illustrate the movement of a supernatural being. While I cannot completely explain God and His supernatural ability, I think His own words do Him justice.

While we exist in the natural world and interact with the creatures of it, God created it all with His word and breath. He put it all into place and set its boundaries and knows the inner workings of each piece of His creation and everything in it. To say we won't believe in Him until we completely understand Him is futile. We will never completely understand Him. Not one person that ever walked or ever will walk this earth will completely understand all that God is. If you have unanswered questions, then do the investigating and don't stop until you get them answered. Persistent prayer should be a part of that.

While we are in this "natural" world, we have a way to be with God. Prayer is a natural conversation that becomes supernatural. He's always calling to us, and He's always speaking to us. God's divine plan to save us was put in place so that we could be with Him and have a relationship with Him (John 10:27-28, Zephaniah 3:17). Therefore prayer extends from the natural realm into the spiritual. It's more than just what we can see, think, hear, and feel. It's not only a way to build a relationship with God; it's a way to bring about a supernatural change to impact our natural world.

For this reason, we can't expect prayer to be exactly like conversations we have with each other. It's not the same. We have an interpreter named the Holy Spirit, and he is translating the words coming out of our mouths when we pray. Prayer with the help of the Holy Spirit involves us in that supernatural world.

We have subtle ways to communicate with each other that don't involve words: our body posture, facial expressions, written words, etc. God can do the same thing, but His platform is so much grander than ours. He has the whole universe to work with. He can reach into one person's life to communicate with another person. He can use anything He wants to communicate with whomever He wants. His communication is more than one-dimensional. It transcends time, thought, emotion, vision, words, and anything else He chooses to transcend. It is unlikely that God is bound by His natural law of physics. His resources are limitless because He creates His own resources. If He can create the Heavens and the Earth out of nothing, how much more can He create to speak to someone He cares about? He can choose a sunset, coffee with a friend, a child's innocent embrace, a song, or even a smile from a stranger to communicate with us. His methods are boundless.

God designed us with deep needs; holes in our hearts. He did it intentionally as they are something only He can fill completely. Good advice is given by William Craig, in his book, *Hard Questions, Real Answers* when he wrote, "When doubts come, then don't try to hide them or pretend they don't exist. Take them to God in prayer and ask Him to help you resolve them."[1] Many of us will spend our entire lives searching for ways to satisfy those needs. The conversations we have, the movies we watch, the music we listen to, and the books we read all reflect common themes that speak to these needs. These needs are often universal: love, relationships, peace, war, good versus evil, suffering, overcoming odds, coming of age, the circle of life, heroism, judgment, survival, and deception.

You don't have to believe in God to know these things exist. They are common to us all. Our Maker left this longing in our spiritual DNA and in our souls, and it is something that binds us all no matter how different we are. These themes are matters of the heart, and that is where God makes His deposits, and that is where He sustains us. It's in the search for answers that He shows Himself to us every day. He is seen by the world daily and still is not recognized (John 14:17). If I want to see Him, I need to look, intentionally, for Him. In order to know if my prayers are answered, then I need to give God credit for the things He is doing every day in my life.

My husband travels a lot. Every time he leaves, I pray that he will return safely, every time. Yet for years, I never thanked God that He brought my husband home safely. One day I realized that I have no idea what God had done to bring my husband home safely. Did He divert a plane from crashing? Did God keep a bomber from crashing into a crowded airport? Did He prevent a car accident so that my husband could travel safely? I have no idea, but that doesn't mean that God had not been working on answering my prayers.

God doesn't sit in a room saying, "Look at me. This is what I've done for you. You asked and wow, look what I had to do to accomplish that." He could, because He can do anything, but in this case, He didn't.

This one time my husband arrived home safely, and I actively thanked God for that occasion. Since then I look for opportunities to thank God for answered prayers. Just because I don't see how something was executed, doesn't mean God wasn't active in answering my prayer. How many times have I prayed for something and received it and I didn't even thank God for delivering what I prayed for?

As I started to thank God more for the good things in my life, I started seeing some of the evidence that I had been overlooking. It's impossible to know everything God does on our behalf, so I choose to give God credit for all the good things in my life, even those things I don't ask for. Furthermore, I learned that it often takes time for God to bring about changes in my heart or the heart of another, so answers don't always come immediately.

I look back at my life and can't help but realize how God's perspective is much different than ours. I can't pretend to know why God allows our hearts and even lives to be broken, but I am convinced from my own experiences that He will help put the pieces back together.

God made us to be connected to Him. While we are not supernatural, we all live in the physical counterpart of a spiritual world. Therefore, in the broadest sense, God touches everyone. The searching for the meaning of life, wanting to be connected to something bigger than ourselves, to love and be loved in return, and all other matters of the heart can be thought of as a spiritual calling from our Maker. The search for these common intangibles is where prayer can provide the direction that leads towards the connection that we were meant to have with God.

CHAPTER 7

SPIRITUAL WARFARE

*"Darkness cannot drive out darkness; only light can do that.
Hate cannot drive out hate; only love can do that."*
—Dr. Martin Luther King, Jr.

*"You're gonna have to serve somebody; well, it may be the devil,
or it may be the Lord, but you're gonna have to serve somebody . . ."*
—Bob Dylan

Although we have battles every day, as plain as day, there are also supernatural battles that we all face. Movies like *Star Wars*, *Harry Potter*, and *The Hobbit* are just a few examples of how our mainstream society deals with supernatural powers. In these movies, the main characters typically represent good and evil.

Our minds and hearts are drawn to these universal themes, and that's why they influence us. These are common themes because whether we admit it or not, we are drawn to a supernatural being who loves us unconditionally and passionately and who has designed us to have a need for Him. He knows we will struggle, suffer, and fall, no matter how good we want our lives to be. The proof that He knows the inner-workings of our hearts, lives, and abilities is the plan He set in place through Jesus so that even though we fall, we can still be with Him for eternity.

In the Old Testament, a sacrifice was needed to make amends for sin.[1] This is akin to needing payment for a debt that is owed and that payment needs to be an absolutely perfect payment according to the conditions of the contract. Nothing less is acceptable. At some point, because of our fallen nature, we will get into debt. Sometimes it's intentional, and sometimes it's unintentional; regardless, our actions have consequences.

For the time being, Satan is leading the rebellion against God. Everyone must choose a team, and no one will be left out. Apathy, unwillingness to make that choice, or being too distracted or too busy to think about this choice doesn't let us off the hook. At the end of our days, we will either be with God or not. Everyone will be given a chance to recognize God, and although that may not require reading the Bible (Romans 1:20), our sin does require payment. Just as light and dark are separate and love and hate are separate, God and our sin are separate. Our sin, which is an act, thought, or way of behaving that violates the nature of God,[2] will not invite the presence of God. Sin will separate us from Him, and that is why God provided the payment needed to reconcile with us or bring us into His presence.

Jesus' "sacrifice" is called that because he chose to give himself in return for our liberation from sin. He is the only appropriate payment for a debt we cannot erase. Our actions, thoughts, and ways of behaving cannot be undone. When our time spent here in this world is over, we will be judged, and there will be things that we will be called to account for. We have all sinned and will continue to sin no matter how much we love God. Jesus did not sin, and that is why he can stand in our place to bridge the gap of separation from God. In that moment, when our time is up, have we paid our debt that allows us past those pearly gates and into God's presence? The only way that happens is to recognize God's plan in Jesus and accept that as our currency (John 14:6).

Satan is captain of Team Evil because he represents everything that opposes God's character. Satan is given footholds in our lives because of our sin, and our ignorance is a staple in the diet of Satan. In an age of reality TV, scientific knowledge, technological advancements, and a reliance on rational thought, many spiritual beliefs are downplayed or seen as unimportant. Satan will use this to his advantage as he recruits people for his rebellion.

In a series of letters written between the devil (Screwtape) and his nephew (Wormwood), C.S. Lewis provides a platform to address serious theological issues, one of them being how to distract people from God.[3] In these letters, Screwtape and Wormwood plot and discuss ways to keep us busy and distracted in any way they can so that we are ignorant and not involved in any spiritual battle. Although C.S. Lewis' narrative might be a satire, a seemingly light-hearted look into trivia, it is an excellent display of truth. Satan will use what distracts us, whether it is our ignorance, pride, apathy, blindness, misguided trust, or anything else he can to prevent us from spending eternity with God. Satan only needs us to spend our entire life not looking to God, acquiring debt in God's economy, and then not accepting the payment that has been provided for us. Being apathetic and unintentional leads us straight to him and, consciously or not, we have signed on the dotted line of Team Satan.

God wants us to choose by intentionally knowing exactly what we are choosing. Satan, on the other hand, masquerades as something he is not, as do all his teammates (2 Corinthians 11:14-15), and will take us whether we choose him intentionally, by our default, by deceit, or by any other means necessary. This would be a sampling of Satan's resume:[4]

- He is the enemy (1 Peter 5:8)
- The evil one (Matthew 6:13)
- The father of lies and a murderer (John 8:44)
- The accuser of God's people (Revelation 12:10)
- The tempter (1 Thessalonians 3:5)
- Proud, wicked, violent, and rebellious (Isaiah 14:12-15)
- A deceiver (Acts 13:10)
- A schemer (Ephesians 6:11)
- A thief (Luke 8:12)

Whether we choose to believe it or not, there is an ongoing battle happening behind the scenes. It's not of this world; it's spiritual. Satan would love for everyone to ignore or scoff at the idea. Refusing to believe in God's plan doesn't make it any less real. Spiritual battles are often fought in our minds and hearts because this is from where our actions flow (Proverbs 4:23).

Most importantly, there is a spiritual battle for our souls. We are a big part of the reason for these battles between God and Satan. The battle for our souls is a love story for the history books. It encompasses all our favorite themes, yet ironically, we can't see it clearly with just our eyes. This battle ripples through time as it impacts us for eternity. It's a battle that decides whether or not, when no more choices are allowed, after all our time is up; if we can go home to the one place we can be loved completely and perfectly . . . or not.

We allow Satan to influence us. How many times have you heard someone say, "The devil made me do it!" when joking about doing something wrong. Our culture relegates demonic influence to something childlike, painting demons as wayward children that nip at the ankles of those they attack. No one is a stranger to the character of Satan and what he represents. He uses our separation and isolation, our own self-deprecating thoughts, our anxieties, our busy-ness, our greed, or whatever we focus on that doesn't line up with who God is.

Satan is the father of lies, the father of deceit, and he will use our very nature to keep us blind and unconnected to love and truth. He, too, is concerned with our hearts, because he knows that where our heart is, so is our treasure (Matthew 6:21). He believes in God, and he knows exactly who God loves. Satan would love to keep as many of us from having a relationship with our Maker as he can. He knows that if he can get us distracted and apathetic to our true purpose in life, which is to worship and praise the true and living God, he wins.

Satan also knows that if we choose to reject God's plan, then there will be a time when God will let us exist without Him. There is a place where God does not go. There is a place where those who do not want Him in their lives get what they want. They also do not enjoy any of the benefits of His nature, His goodness, truth, and light, but most of all His love. There is a place where Satan does pour forth all of his evilness on God's loved ones for eternity without God's protection and influence (Psalm 9:17, 2 Thessalonians 1:9, Matthew 25:41).

That is not where I choose to be. I want my eternal destination to be in a place where I'm surrounded by love, truth, and goodness, not just for me but for everyone. God loves us all and wants us all to live with Him eternally. He chooses not to do things, to not intervene or not give because His perspective is eternal. His financial plan doesn't get us to retirement, but through eternity. He is concerned with where we all will be forever. Even though Satan is allowed to roam the Earth, God is active on our behalf. Maybe He allows Satan to roam because there would be no choice without something to choose between.[5] What I do know is that Satan works hard to deceive us and has worked for generations to do what he can to see that we are blind to the truth. He's been doing it since he spoke with Adam and Eve in the Garden of Eden.

In the movie *The Matrix*, people were sleeping while dreaming of lives being created in their minds to keep them distracted from what was really happening to them. Are we mindlessly living our lives day to day without an eternal purpose? Are we living lives that seem unfulfilling? The storyline in *The Matrix* showed that suffering is a necessary element of our humanity and this is often true in real life. Suffering can bring out the best and the worst in us all.

While under the rule of the Roman empire, Ephesus was a prosperous port city. During that time, some suggest that it was "second only to Rome as a cosmopolitan center of culture and commerce."[6]

Paul wrote to the Ephesians while he was most likely imprisoned in Rome.[7] As a Roman citizen (Acts 22:28) Paul would have been familiar with Roman warriors, their legions, weapons, and power. Although it isn't explicitly stated in the Bible that Paul is referring to an actual Roman soldier when he writes about spiritual armor, it could be that Paul uses a comparison to the Roman soldiers to share a spiritual truth. He has provided a tangible, visual picture for the Ephesians he was writing to in order to help them understand and remember a spiritual, invisible truth.

COME FILL THIS PLACE

The Armor of God: Ephesians 6:10-18

"Finally, be strong in the Lord and in his mighty power. Put on the full armor of God, so that you can take your stand against the devil's schemes. For our struggle is not against flesh and blood, but against the rulers, against the authorities, against the powers of this dark world and against the spiritual forces of evil in the heavenly realms. Therefore put on the full armor of God, so that when the day of evil comes, you may be able to stand your ground, and after you have done everything, to stand. Stand firm then, with the belt of truth buckled around your waist, with the breastplate of righteousness in place, and with your feet fitted with the readiness that comes from the gospel of peace. In addition to all this, take up the shield of faith, with which you can extinguish all the flaming arrows of the evil one. Take the helmet of salvation and the sword of the Spirit, which is the word of God.

And pray in the Spirit on all occasions with all kinds of prayers and requests. With this in mind, be alert and always keep on praying for all the Lord's people."

This verse implies that the fight isn't in our cultural differences and beliefs or in our political and personal opinions. Our battle isn't with one another; it's with what separates us from God.

When I was in Russia, the girls we visited wrote verses from the Bible on index cards and used clear tape to make them more durable. They would use these cards to memorize scripture. I remember being touched by how much they valued God's word. I also remember how so many people told me that if I wanted to hear from God that I needed to read and memorize scripture, but I didn't really understand how valuable that would be.

For some reason, these index cards, covered in clear tape with handwritten words, impacted me profoundly. I began making little laminated scripture verse cards to help me remember verses. Having a notoriously bad memory, I also employ the use of acronyms to help me memorize scriptures. My personal keychain of memory verses is overwhelming with the number of verses attached that cover all my insecurities. It's by knowing God's word that I am able to fight my spiritual battles because it counters Satan's most useful tools: lies and deception. God's words also help me stay focused on the real issue as Satan also loves to distract and immobilize.

When I was much younger, I became unhappy with my life as it was and, seeing no way out, I wanted it to end. When I felt that I had lost the ability to achieve those dreams I had as a teen, I became hopeless and acted out with self-destructive behavior. I put myself in many dangerous situations and acted recklessly without much regard for my welfare or the welfare of others.

At this time in my life, I started going out with an older guy who assaulted me while I was incoherently drunk. I never gave my verbal consent, so I consider it a violation. Putting myself in a situation that was harmful is something I regret to this day. Yet, at that time, because of my brokenness and his threat to expose me, I remained in a dysfunctional relationship. It became a warped relationship in which at times I felt loved and at other times, I felt immensely ashamed of what I had become.

I thought I would remain a virgin until married, yet as I hit my later teens, things changed. Something significant was taken from me without my consent. That is partly why having choices means so much to me. That's why being built up and not torn down means so much to me. That's why I try to keep people close to me who choose to help me.

When I wanted to memorize this particular verse on spiritual warfare, I realized that Satan always wants to *rape* and pillage. He wants to take our security and hope from us. These are strong words and ideas, but in the context of a spiritual battle for our eternal souls, it seems appropriate to me, and they helped me to remember what Paul was trying to teach in Ephesians 6:10-18. In verse twelve, he says this:

> *"For our struggle is not against flesh and blood, but against the rulers, against the authorities, against the powers of this dark world and against the spiritual forces of evil in the heavenly realms."*

COME FILL THIS PLACE

This is how I remember it:

Our struggle is not against flesh and blood but against RAPE.

R: rulers, A: authorities, P: powers of this dark world, E: spiritual forces of evil in the heavenly realms.

In my own personal journey, I want to stand against RAPE as well as protect others from having something stolen from them. This is a matter of life and death to me, and whether I am aware of a specific battle, whether a loved one is aware or anyone else for that matter, I pray that God will protect us all from being assaulted by an enemy that is intent on stealing from us when we are unaware. We may be unaware of the spiritual battles around us, but we don't have to be. Prayer protects us. God's word protects us.

During my experiences in Russia, this verse gave me something to focus on while I was praying about what was happening to me. Although I am sure there are other concepts used to help explain the visual Paul gives to the Ephesians, I am going to share one I am very familiar with as it was taught to me many years ago. I found it very valuable in helping to remember the different pieces of armor and their significance. Understanding cultural meaning and context does help make sense of the Bible, but it isn't required to understand the things God wants you to know. In prayer, we can ask God, through the Holy Spirit, to give us understanding (2 Corinthians 2:11).

For now, because it's what helped me remember the verse, I will share what I learned.

> *"Stand firm then, with the belt of truth buckled around your waist, with the breastplate of righteousness in place"* (Ephesians 5:14).

Many who would have read Paul's letter would have been very familiar with how Roman soldiers dressed for battle. Their belt is what supports and secures all their weapons and equipment they need close by at all times.[8] Truth is everything God is and represents. Satan is not. We cannot lie, deceive, or misrepresent and expect God to answer prayers that support that. Everything God does and asks us to do is built around truth. It's the foundation that faith is built on.

The second part of this verse is "the breastplate of righteousness." As a soldier, vital organs must be protected.[9] The heart is an organ we have talked about so although the Romans soldiers wore actual breastplates to protect their physical hearts from attack, Paul could have used this metaphor to tell us that in spiritual battle, our hearts are vital and must be protected.

Our actions and words are a reflection of what is in our hearts. Living with a belief that good will ultimately prevail and living in a way God asks us to live is essential. Satan cannot demolish us with his attacks if we protect ourselves with God's Word. I don't think anyone has regretted living a virtuous, right, just, blameless, and honorable life. When we live as righteously as we can the world can see God in our lives. It's when we move past our own attitudes and towards taking on something spiritual that battles are won on God's behalf. He asks us to clothe ourselves not with satin or silk, gold or diamonds; although impressive, these things do not reflect the character of God. They do not help us to stand in His battle.

In a letter written to the Galatians, Paul talks about living in the spirit and what that looks like. Galatians 5:22-23 tells us:

> *"But the fruit of the Spirit is love, joy, peace, forbearance, kindness, goodness, faithfulness, gentleness and self-control. Against such things there is no law."*

We can never go wrong when these qualities are reflected in our lives. For me, this takes prayer. I cannot live this way without God's influence and strength. Although I am learning and growing and modeling my life after God's character, my selfishness makes me stumble. It's by asking for these things that I see the Holy

Spirit working in my life. It may not be immediate, but, these are things God always will want to give, in any situation, no matter what. I have confidence when I ask for these things that my prayers will bear fruit. These qualities also protect us from Satan's attacks on our hearts.

Fear, bitterness, anger, lack of forgiveness, pride, or anything that opposes God's nature, will leave little room for love, joy, peace, and a package of figs. Yes, my acronym for Galatians 5:22-23 is: Love, Joy, Peace, and P-patience (forbearance), K-kindness, G-goodness, F-faithfulness, G-gentleness, and S-Self-control. I want to live with Love, Joy, Peace and a PKG of FIGS. We are given more freedom to affect others when we ask for these things.[10] He loves us all; even in ways we can't fathom (Psalm 107:8-9, Psalm 36:5-6).

A continuation of Paul's armor can be found in Ephesians 6:15:

> *"and with our feet fitted with the readiness that comes from the gospel of peace."*

A soldier must protect his feet. It is how he moves and navigates battles. His feet provide balance and a good foundation.[11] Without feet ready to move, in any direction, it doesn't matter how many weapons a soldier has strapped to his belt, he will be ineffective.

Spiritually, this is what God's Word does for us as well. So much can be said about this short statement, but essentially His Word is the foundation that all our physical movement should be built upon. It's also the foundation that our prayers should be built upon if we are to affect others spiritually. If we are asked to stand, wouldn't we need something to stand on? Satan uses deceit and trickery to try to lead us to places we should not be. If each of our steps is placed on God's truth, we cannot get lost, and our footing will be solid. Jesus modeled this in Matthew 4:1-4 when being tempted, he responded to each of the devil's half-truths with God's Word.

Paul continues by saying in Ephesians 6:16:

"In addition to all this, take up the shield of faith, with which you can extinguish all the flaming arrows of the evil one."

In addition to a belt of truth and a breastplate of righteousness, we need a shield of faith. Roman soldiers would have needed their shields to protect themselves from deadly attacks coming quickly from any direction. They were trained to move it swiftly and efficiently without much reasoning and thought. Moving their shields would have been reactive, shielding them from danger coming from any direction. They also moved as a group and put their shields together to form a wall of protection. When arrows came from above, they could huddle together and form a turtle shape with shields above and around the sides, working together to form a strong barrier.[12]

Likewise, faith is binding. It allows us to work in community with God and with others. When we seek God and look to love others, hearts change, actions change, and lives are changed.

In a letter to the Hebrews, Paul writes about this faith in action:

"Now faith is confidence in what we hope for and assurance about what we do not see" (Hebrews 11:1).

Roman soldiers had to be confident that their shield would protect them, and they had to have assurance that it would work against whatever attacks came. It moves because a battle doesn't come from the same direction and in the same way every time. Otherwise, they could just stand behind an immovable barrier like a wall. Paul may have used this example because we are asked to move in this world. Whether we do it intentionally or not, unless we are hermits we affect others.

COME FILL THIS PLACE

Everyone has a place where they impact others: parents affect children, teachers affect students, and co-workers affect co-workers. Just by going about our daily business, lives are changed and influenced because of the relationships we have and how we connect. Our spiritual shield of faith can be moved around to help protect others who cannot raise their own or side by side to widen our range of protection. This is done through prayer, relying on our confidence in what we hope for and our belief in something unseen. When we are standing on God's word, prayers are answered, Satan's flaming arrows fall to the ground, and we are not consumed or torn down by the evil or the wickedness of others.

Moving a shield around requires an observant, open, and flexible mind. I intentionally try to be observant to what God is doing in my life. This means focusing on Him, and I try to keep my mind open and flexible as I seek to understand all that God is, how He is working in my life and in the lives of others, and how I need to respond. His ways are not ours (Isaiah 55:8-9), and this understanding takes prayer in faith.

Paul continues with his next instruction in Ephesians 6:17-18:

"Take the helmet of salvation and the sword of the Spirit, which is the word of God. And pray in the Spirit on all occasions with all kinds of prayers and requests."

For obvious reasons, the helmet protects the warrior's most vital organ, his mind. We can picture warriors on a battlefield, helmet in place just leaving enough opening for his eyes to see and for his mouth to breathe and speak.[13] This is a picture of a helmet worn in physical battle, but many spiritual battles play out in our minds. If evil can overcome our thoughts, if we are consumed with burning thoughts of bitterness, envy, greed, jealousness, maliciousness, and ill-intent, we can feel as though we are under attack. In many cases, we then feel justified to "go on the attack." Our actions flow from our hearts to our minds and control our bodies. Since our thoughts control our actions, it makes sense that salvation is placed there. This is why salvation is not rooted in emotion.[14] For each individual, their salvation depends on their mind; on a choice, they will need to make before they die.

The helmet of salvation is partnered with the only offensive weapon in our spiritual armor, the sword of the spirit, which is the word of God.

Our salvation is built on God's Word, so this partnership would make sense in Paul's reference. Paul's use of the word *sword* is thought of as referring to the two-edged sword that the soldier would have used.[15] Many people feel justified in using God's Word to attack each other verbally and feel that they are doing so because Paul references it as being a sword: a weapon. But they don't take into account the next few words. It is the sword of the Spirit, not the sword of Stacy Dietz or a sword belonging to any other natural being.

This sword is wielded by a spiritual being that God places in the heart of every person who believes in His Son. I prefer to think of letting the Holy Spirit use God's sword to attack the enemy when it strikes my heart and mind. When I battle in my mind, I use His Word (this is why my memory verse keychain is so large) to change my thoughts, to realign them to truth and away from the lies told by an ungodly influence. This is a spiritual battle based on my faith in the hope that God is who He says He is, and a belief in things I cannot see. I prefer to let the scriptures that come from my mouth help build up others and not attack them. If they are people that have given me permission to hold them accountable in their faith, then I can remind them of things they already know (2 Timothy 3:16).

As in anything, the more we know and are given, the more we are held to account (Luke 12:48). Our wisdom and understanding are shown by the way we live our lives (James 3:13). I believe as we grow, we need to hold ourselves to account and not use God's words to "stab" others into submission. At the end of my life, I will not be accounting for anyone's life but my own. Can I stand against evil? Can I stand against RAPE? Most certainly. It is a necessity. Yet, in our everyday conversations, we can choose to use scripture to build up those around us, to help teach and correct and not attack, "cut", and malign.

The last thing Paul mentions in Ephesians 6:17 is:

"pray in the Spirit on all occasions with all kinds of prayers and requests."

The helmet, sword, and prayer are all closely linked together with "*and.*"

Our thoughts are vital. What we choose to do with them is of the utmost importance to fighting battles spiritually. Our prayers are tied to our faith and tied to the action of the *Holy Spirit,* who we can rely on because the Word of God is truth. We are asked to pray in the spirit so that the *Holy Spirit* can act with his sword, which is the Word of God. It is this sword that changes hearts and affects destinies, but it is not wielded by us to attack another person, it is used by a spiritual being. The action we are to take while we are standing against evil is to pray on all occasions.

I have faith that the more I reflect His character by letting the Holy Spirit work in my heart, cutting and killing all the things that separate me from God or keep me from living a righteous life, the more I use my shield of faith to love, protect, and build up others, the more battles I will be able to stand firm in.

CHAPTER 8

HOLY SPIRIT

"May it be a light to you in dark places, when all other lights go out."
—J.R.R. Tolkien, The Fellowship of the Ring

"As he was about to climb yet another dune, his heart whispered,
'Be aware of the place where you are brought to tears.
That's where I am, and that's where your treasure is.'"
—Paulo Coelho, The Alchemist

I like to pray through scripture. It helps me to focus my thoughts on what God wants for me. This is particularly helpful when I am struggling with my own emotions or having a hard time focusing. People sometimes feel like they have to talk to God the same way they talk to an English teacher; in language that is grammatically and structurally perfect. I thank God that's not the case. God doesn't need us to use precise and perfect words when praying (Romans 8:26). Many women I have spoken to over the years shared that they felt inadequate in coming to God with their prayers. None of us needs to be adequate or perfect because God has deposited the Holy Spirit into our hearts and he is more than adequate, and he is perfect.

COME FILL THIS PLACE

In Paul's letter to the church in Corinth, he writes:

> *"It is God who enables us, along with you, to stand firm for Christ. He has commissioned us, and He has identified us as His own by placing the Holy Spirit in our hearts as the first installment that guarantees everything He has promised us . . ."* (2 Corinthians 1:21-22, New Living Translation).

This installment, the Holy Spirit, is the part of the community of God that lives in us. We must be aware that God wants to make other deposits as well. That is why we need to open our hearts and minds when we pray, allowing God to make the deposits, that on our own, we might overlook or misunderstand.

The Holy Spirit works in community with God and with us to help us communicate more effectively with Him. Many times, scripture mentions the Holy Spirit (Jude 1:20, Acts 2:4, Luke 4:1). This means that the Holy Spirit is something that is in addition to what we are. It can be a complicated aspect of our relationship with God, so let's break it down to *who, what, when, where, how, and why*.

WHO IS THE HOLY SPIRIT?

The Holy Spirit is the third part of a community of three that God, the Father and Jesus are a part of. All are divine, and all are God. God abides in a triune community, commonly taught as God the Father, God the son (Jesus), and the Spirit of God (Holy Spirit). God never meant for us to live alone and He says this very clearly in Genesis 2:18:

> *"It is not good for the man to be alone. I will make a helper suitable for him."*

So it shouldn't be surprising that He is not alone either.

Understanding God's triune nature is extremely important and can be complex. The Bible says, in 2 Corinthians 3:17,

Holy Spirit

> *"Now the Lord is the Spirit, and where the Spirit of the Lord is, there is freedom."*

The Holy Spirit is not a separate God; he is God.[1] He is not a vague, invisible wisp of smoke. One example that is commonly used to explain a triune nature is water. Water is a single compound that can exist in three states, liquid, ice, and gas,[2] God exists in three different entities. Another example that helps to make sense of this complexity is a math problem. Many might be thinking of the triune nature of God as $1 + 1 + 1 = 3$, which causes confusion. The equation $1 \times 1 \times 1 = 1$ is a better way to think about it.[3] Although examples can help with understanding an important concept, it certainly cannot completely tell us how impactful the Holy Spirit is to us, and our prayer lives.

There are some things that require faith. In Hebrews 11:1 it says:

> *"Now faith is confidence in what we hope for and assurance about what we do not see."*

I cannot completely describe who the Holy Spirit is in its entirety, but I can say with confidence that when you seek God and spend time with Him, He will reveal to you the things He would like you to know. We cannot insist that God fits into our understanding. He doesn't, but He can and wants to give us wisdom so that our understanding of Him grows (James 1:5, Proverbs 2:6).

WHAT DOES THE HOLY SPIRIT DO?

What is important for our prayer life and our life, in general, are two things: the Holy Spirit empowers us (Acts 1:8, 2 Timothy 1:7), and He equips us with spiritual gifts (1 Corinthians 12:4).

Power is described as the capacity to do something, strength, or the authority to act.[4] I don't always feel particularly powerful, but I do feel that because of God, I have the capacity to do something, and He gives me the authority to act. He's equipped me to do what He wants me to do. It's through prayer that I gain strength and know the details of how to act in my daily life, in what areas I have the authority to act, and how to use my gifts. It's through prayer and through the Holy Spirit that I can understand what God would like me to see.

> *"For who among men knows the thoughts of man except his own spirit within him? So too, no one knows the thoughts of God except the Spirit of God. We have not received the spirit of the world, but the Spirit who is from God, that we may understand what God has freely given us"* (1 Corinthians 2:11-12).

The Holy Spirit has many attributes. Here is a short list of them:

- He convicts us of sin — John 16:8
- He teaches and reminds us — John 14:26
- He guides us into all truth — John 16:13
- He bears fruit through us — Galatians 5:22-23
- He is with us — John 16:7
- He reveals and enlightens — 1 Corinthians 2:11-12, 14
- He testifies — John 15:26
- He guides — Romans 8:14
- He speaks — 1 Corinthians 2:13
- He gives instructions — Acts 1:1-2
- He contends — Genesis 6:3
- He commands — Acts 8:28-29
- He intercedes — Romans 8:26
- He sends workers — Acts 13:4
- He calls — Revelations 22:17
- He works — 1 Corinthians 12:11

- He can be grieved   Isaiah 63:10, Ephesians 4:30
- He confirms the truth   Romans 9:1

WHEN DID THE HOLY SPIRIT SHOW UP?

The very first verse in the Bible tells us:

> *"In the beginning God created the heavens and the earth. Now the earth was formless and empty, darkness was over the surface of the deep, and the Spirit of God was hovering over the waters"* (Genesis 1:1).

In the beginning God was not alone. The Spirit of God was hovering over the waters. It is this Spirit that has been deposited in our hearts. It is this Spirit that provides wisdom, understanding, advice, gives strength, knowledge, and reverence (Isaiah 11:2).

When Jesus gave his disciples the task of preaching the gospel to the entire world, they had absolutely no power to carry it out until the Holy Spirit came (Luke 24:49). In the same way, if we hope to accomplish what God desires in our lives, we need to see Him as our source of power and strength. If we want to affect others for God, it would be wise to pray before we speak and act.

In God's economy, our sin requires payment so that we can be with Him. Jesus is that payment. God, knowing that we could not possibly live out His laws perfectly, gave us a perfect substitute. We just have to choose to accept that as truth (Acts 2:38). When we do, God deposits the Holy Spirit into our hearts.

WHERE DOES THE HOLY SPIRIT LIVE AND *HOW* IS HE GIVEN?

Since God deals with our hearts, it makes sense that He would make a most valuable deposit there. Where the Holy Spirit resides is so closely linked to *How* he is given, because only God can make that deposit into our hearts. Scripture says:

> *"I will ask the Father, and He will give you another Helper, that He may be with you forever; that is the Spirit of truth, whom the world cannot receive, because it does not see Him or know Him, but you know Him because He abides with you and will be in you" (John 14:16-17). "Do you not know that your bodies are temples of the Holy Spirit, who is in you, whom you have received from God?" (1 Corinthians 6:19).*

It may seem strange that God can live inside us. Truthfully, I cannot entirely explain the mechanics of that. Many times when I pray the sensation that comes over me first, happens internally. Although sometimes God speaks through His physical creations, His Word can affect me emotionally. Although God is not restricted in how He works with us, the first place that He usually starts is with our hearts. The more we ask, seek, knock, search, question, and pursue God, the more we will find and the more we will understand:

> *"For I know the plans I have for you," declares the Lord, "plans to prosper you and not to harm you, plans to give you hope and a future. Then you will call on me and come and pray to me, and I will listen to you. You will seek me and find me when you seek me with all your heart. I will be found by you," declares the Lord . . ." (Jeremiah 29:11-14).*

WHY DO WE NEED THE HOLY SPIRIT?

We are not divine creatures. Our DNA is purely natural, not containing an ounce of divinity. Yet, we are treasured and loved by a God who wants to be our Father and so much more. The scripture says:

> *"For those who are led by the Spirit of God are the children of God. The Spirit you received does not make you slaves, so that you live in fear again; rather, the Spirit you received brought about your adoption to son ship. And by him we cry, "Abba, Father." The Spirit himself testifies with our*

spirit that we are God's children. Now if we are children, then we are heirs—heirs of God and co-heirs with Christ, if indeed we share in his sufferings in order that we may also share in his glory" (Romans 8:14).

As God's adopted ones, we become His children. As His children, we are promised to be heirs, which means we are promised an eternal life with Him. We are also under His protection, provision, and care while here on earth. Along with all these many privileges we are given under His care, we also have responsibilities that line up with representing Him well and showing others His character through how we live our lives. Many children are a reflection of their parents and their activities. As we become a part of God's family, we should reflect all that He is to the best of our abilities because of the love He has shown us and because of our love for Him.

When we believe that Jesus is who he says he is, God's seal, the Holy Spirit, is deposited into our heart. A seal is a device or substance that is used to join two things together to prevent them from separating. It is also used as a piece of wax, lead, or other material with an individual design stamped into it, and attached to a document, to show that it has come from the person who claims to have issued it.[5] When God places His seal of the Holy Spirit in our hearts, it is intentional and has purpose. We are bound to Him for eternity, and we are now a representative of Him with His individual design stamped into our hearts.[6] In Ephesians 1:13-14, it says:

> *"When you believed, you were marked in him with a seal, the promised Holy Spirit, who is a deposit guaranteeing our inheritance until the redemption of those who are God's possession, to the praise of his glory."*

When Paul wrote this letter to the church of Ephesus, the readers of his letters would have understood his reference of being marked with a seal. It was used often in the ancient world.[7] Once sealed, it became an official document that carried with it the distinct authority of the one sending it. It was not to be opened until it was delivered to its intended recipient.[8] Our hearts are the soft substance on which God would like to make His omniscient impression and individual mark. It is the deposit of the Holy Spirit that gives us authenticity, ownership, and authority to represent God. It is through the Holy Spirit that our inheritance is assured and becomes permanent. In regards to our prayer life, Paul states in Romans 8:26-27 that we have an advocate:

> *"In the same way, the Spirit helps us in our weakness. We do not know what we ought to pray for, but the Spirit himself intercedes for us through wordless groans. And he who searches our hearts knows the mind of the Spirit, because the Spirit intercedes for God's people in accordance with the will of God."*

Two things mentioned here are very important for our prayer life. The first is that we do not know what we ought to pray for, yet the Holy Spirit intercedes for us. Second, the Spirit intercedes in accordance with the will of God. We may not always know exactly what or how to pray, but that will not make our prayers wasted, useless, or unneeded because the Holy Spirit intercedes for us. What is helpful is to have hearts that are concerned with the will of God. When the Holy Spirit is deposited in our hearts, our lives become a cooperative effort in allowing God to work in us and coming to a fuller understanding of who He is and what that means for us.

Scripture reinforces this point:

> *"So what shall I do? I will pray with my spirit, but I will also pray with my understanding; I will sing with my spirit, but I will also sing with my understanding"* (1 Corinthians 14:15).

That deposit also requires action. We aren't given something so that we can hide, conceal, or pretend it doesn't exist. Since God is about community, His deposits are not meant for the hard steel of an unapproachable bank vault. His deposits are meant for millions of permeable, moldable, moveable hearts that affect other hearts for His glory. This means we are meant to move around with the Holy Spirit in our hearts affecting others so that they, too, can become adopted and loved for eternity. It's a natural instinct that when we come across something we love and treasure that we share our find with others. Testifying about God is simply that, sharing what we know about Him with others. God is in charge of changing a person's heart, not us. We are just representatives.

The scriptures say:

> "But you, dear friends, by building yourselves up in your most holy faith and praying in the Holy Spirit, keep yourselves in God's love as you wait for the mercy of our Lord Jesus Christ to bring you to eternal life. Be merciful to those who doubt; save others by snatching them from the fire; to others show mercy . . ." (Jude 1:20-23).

Our faith is meant to be extended to others with mercy, not judgment or in an attempt to control.

I often think of my in-laws when they were just a family I hung out with. I went through a period of rebellion and thought swearing constantly meant I had freedom to say whatever I pleased. What it really showed everyone around me was that I lacked self-control and respect or care for those around me who would be offended by my words. Ignorant of this, I often showed off and did this even in their company. They did not judge me. They didn't insult me nor did they condone my behavior. They just continued to be the best ambassadors they could be. As they continued to love me and represent God well, I began to investigate what that meant. Eventually, God convicted me of my behavior, which has lasted far longer than a scolding from a judgmental person. I have come to understand that with more understanding, comes more responsibility. With responsibility comes more privilege. I wasn't at a point of understanding this principle at that time in my life, but I would expect my in-laws to say something now if my behavior did not line up with my current understanding.

COME FILL THIS PLACE

Many people are concerned with how every person will be given a chance to know what God has done even if they have never been exposed to the Bible. I believe that although it's good to be concerned with things like this, we are primarily responsible for our own decisions. Within our circle of influence, we can testify to what we believe to be the truth. Wanting everyone to be reached causes our circles of influence to widen. We can do what we can and trust that God has a plan for every single heart to be given a chance to choose truth, no matter how He reaches them (Hebrews 2:1-4).

We testify to who God is by living lives that affirm His presence in it. We demonstrate our faith by having our lives show evidence of the Holy Spirit living in our hearts. In the hottest of pressure cooker situations, in the most tragic of moments, in the most unbearable times in our lives, in the courthouse moments, do we make the declaration for God or for ourselves?

When my mother-in-law chose to thank God for giving her son nineteen years of life she was declaring evidence of her love for God in her courthouse moment. Those moments look different for everyone, based on their authentic understanding and time spent with God. She and the entire family's actions during that difficult time were built on a strong foundation of prayer. As mature Christians, both my mother- and father-in-law showed me, in their courthouse moments, hearts that had a deep and eternal understanding of who God is and whose care they believe their son is in for eternity. On that day, I am grateful that I saw their love for God because it changed the trajectory of my life.

I started with this verse when I began this chapter, and I will finish this section with it.

> *"It is God who enables us, along with you, to stand firm for Christ. He has commissioned us, and He has identified us as His own by placing the Holy Spirit in our hearts as the first installment that guarantees everything He has promised us"* (2 Corinthians 1:21-22, New Living Translation).

Prayers can change lives. Persistently seeking God in prayer can change anyone's life. All it takes is a beginning. One intentional step leads to another, and then another. I pray that this book encourages you to take a deeper dive into your own spiritual lives. Likewise, I acknowledge that my journey isn't over. I'm excited to see where God takes me next.

CHAPTER 9

WE HAVE A MODEL: THE LORD'S PRAYER

> *"Action without vision is only passing time, vision without action is merely day dreaming, but vision with action can change the world."*
> —Nelson Mandela

> *"The improvement of understanding is for two ends: first, our own increase of knowledge; secondly, to enable us to deliver that knowledge to others."*
> —John Locke

It's clear that God wants us to pray. It is mentioned over 600 times throughout scripture.[1] While we don't always have proof that we can see or measure, it's evident in scripture that our prayers are answered from reading verses such as James 5:16, 1 John 3:22, and John 15:7.

Jesus prayed many times during his earthly ministry. When asked how to pray, he gives a model in the form of what is commonly known as *The Lord's Prayer*. It can be found in both the book of Luke and Matthew.

COME FILL THIS PLACE

In the book of Matthew, *The Lord's Prayer* is not the first thing Jesus teaches. There are so many things that lay the groundwork for effective, meaningful prayer. It's not only about closing yourself off, sitting in a private place, and setting up the perfect surroundings. Jesus first talks about the position of our hearts by opening his Sermon on the Mount with what has become known as the Beatitudes (Matthew 5:3-10):

1. Blessed are the poor in spirit, for theirs is the kingdom of heaven.
2. Blessed are those who mourn, for they will be comforted.
3. Blessed are the meek, for they will inherit the earth.
4. Blessed are those who hunger and thirst for righteousness, for they will be filled.
5. Blessed are the merciful, for they will be shown mercy.
6. Blessed are the pure in heart, for they will see God.
7. Blessed are the peacemakers, for they will be called children of God.
8. Blessed are those who are persecuted because of righteousness, for theirs is the kingdom of heaven.

Jesus is teaching them that God cares for the poor in spirit, the ones who are mourning, the meek, those who hunger and thirst for righteousness, those who are merciful, the peacekeepers, and those who are persecuted because of [God's] righteousness. Jesus names these types of conditions so that people will know how deeply God cares for those in need and those who recognize their need for God and are searching. He answers those who call out for bigger and better things.

Bryon Yawn, in his video, *What is the Significance of the Beatitudes?*, adds another caveat to the discussion by saying that the Beatitudes were not simply platitudes or ways to live but that they were grenades detonated to attack the cultural thinking of those listening to Jesus speak.[2] These bombs were meant to attack the cultural thinking that self-righteousness or any "prized virtue" was enough to attain God's blessing.[3] I find this idea thought provoking because so many of the things

We Have a Model: The Lord's Prayer

Jesus did, were contrary to the belief system of the culture he lived in. He did not come as a conquering king as many expected the messiah to be; instead, he came as a servant.

A cornerstone in my life's journey and a most impactful concept in regard to prayer are the words *"Blessed are those who are pure in heart, for they will see God."* The word "pure" is defined as "not mixed with any other substance or material, without any extraneous and unnecessary elements, free of any contamination."[4] Often the Bible uses this word to describe a moral or ethical condition. We are asked to "be pure" of heart, not perfect in heart, and God will reveal himself to us.

I often pray that my children, their children, their children's children, and as many generations as I can picture will see God. I know if they see Him, He is working in their hearts.

Some of my family grew up in Hawaii, and so I'm very familiar with the culture. Recently I was interested in a video of a lady reciting the Lord's Prayer in Hawaiian. I don't speak the language, but I love hearing it and often listen to Hawaiian music as it just seems familiar and comforting. The Hawaiian culture and its people can be quite spiritual. Perhaps people living on what is essentially a huge anchored boat in the middle of an extensive body of water are innately aware that they are a small part of something that is much larger than them.

In the video when this lady came onstage, at first, she sang the Lord's Prayer in English. It was subdued and reverent as she stood still while she held the microphone. When she finished, she put the microphone down and began chanting and singing the Lord's Prayer in Hawaiian.[5]

It was powerful. She used her hands all the way to her fingertips to communicate. It became more than a song. It was passionate, and it was pure. I didn't understand the words themselves, but I saw how her body language changed. She stood taller, she looked more powerful. Her words were passionate, and it was clear that she was single-minded about what she was communicating. Her conversation was uncontaminated and natural, and because of that, it touched my heart. Not every prayer is like this, but if more of them were, how much more clearly could we see God?

Jesus continues to say:

> *"(you are) blessed when people insult, persecute you and falsely say all kinds of evil because of me. We should rejoice and be glad, because our reward in heaven is great"* (Matthew 5:11).

This doesn't say we are blessed because of the suffering we go through. Instead it says that we are blessed because of who He is. If we are making bad decisions and are treated badly because of that, we can't blame our faith. That isn't what Jesus is talking about.

He continues:

> *"You are the salt of the earth. But if the salt loses its saltiness, how can it be made salty again? It is no longer good for anything, except to be thrown out and trampled underfoot"* (Matthew 5:13).

He continues in verses 14-16:

> *"You are the light of the world. A town built on a hill cannot be hidden. Neither do people light a lamp and put it under a bowl. Instead they put it on its stand, and it gives light to everyone in the house. In the same way, let your light shine before others, that they may see your good deeds and glorify your Father in heaven."*

These scriptures illustrate that our purpose in life is two-fold. One, we have a purpose, which will affect others, and two, we have a light that we should shine so brightly that it brings others to glorify God. Much like moths unable to resist any light shining in the darkness of our summer nights, we do not bring others to know who God is, the light emanating from us does. That light becomes an irresistible attraction that some people won't be able to resist.

Conversely, are we living our lives in a way that doesn't contaminate the light we hold? Have we, as vessels of that light, spent time cleaning our own window panes so that others can see the light? Or are we too busy leading others, clouded by our own judgment, in the direction of our own making, without asking God where to go or what to say or how to act? It's our willingness to live a certain way that shows how much we love and respect God. Perhaps this is why Jesus mentioned that if others treat us with malice because of who we follow and not because of who we are, then great will our reward be. They are attacking the light we carry, not the vessel. This means they can see it and choose to reject it. God rewards us for this.

This brings us to Jesus explaining his mission here on Earth. In the New International Version translation of the Bible, it's headed *The Fulfillment of the Law*. Jesus says:

> "Do not think that I have come to abolish the Law or the Prophets; I have not come to abolish them but to fulfill them." Verse 19: ". . . anyone who sets aside one of the least of these commands and teaches others accordingly will be called least in the kingdom of heaven, but whoever practices and teaches these commands will be called great in the kingdom of heaven. For I tell you that unless your righteousness surpasses that of the Pharisees and the teachers of the law, you will certainly not enter the kingdom of heaven" (Matthew 5:17-19).

Simply put, we are asked to live a certain way. We cannot live our lives holding out our hands to receive from God what we will not give to others. That's not why He gives. That's not why he answers our prayers. He does not enable greediness and hoarding. With this said, he understands that not one of us will live in perfection, so Jesus tells us he has come to fulfill where we fall short. When we look to the

Word of God and allow the Holy Spirit to work in our lives, God builds a bridge to cover the gap between being the best vessel we can be (to help others see God) and being the perfect vessel (in which that very special light deserves to be carried). We alone cannot shine that light, because that light is not us, but the presence of God.

God works in the community of the Father, Jesus and the Holy Spirit. Since God works in community for a community, shouldn't we? Shouldn't some of our prayers, if not all of our prayers, be concerned with community in some way?

I did a simple "most common word used in the Bible" internet search and found that (not counting words like a, the, is, etc.) the most common words are consistent with God's desire to share who He is and to be in community with us. Depending on the version of the Bible used the counts are roughly as follows: Lord[6] (7,000-8,000), God (4,293), Man (2,747), Israel (2,509), and People (2,271).[7] Many of the words that top the list of frequently used have to do with community and identity.[8] Some of the most used words in the Bible aren't about our hearts or about our actions, both of which are extremely important to God. Perhaps I'm oversimplifying the issue by using a simple word count but the use of these words show us that God is interested in sharing who He is, the relationship He wants to have, and that we are important to Him. He is continually reaching out to us, desiring for us all to live in community with Him.

The last two things Jesus asks us to do before he begins to teach about prayer is to love our enemy and to give to the needy. Both are communal, and both serve as a transition to Jesus talking about prayer. These are two special issues dealing with community that will require prayer to fulfill.

To love our enemy requires sacrifice in ways we are not naturally inclined to do. Supernaturally, though, when we ask for the ability to love and forgive those who harm us, prayers are answered. Sometimes they are answered with an immediate change of heart. Sometimes they are answered only after asking patiently and persistently. As we work on our own heart issues, we are assured that our prayers will be answered because it is something we are asked to do and Jesus fulfills that law when we cannot. God works supernaturally to enable us to do extra-ordinary things, no matter who we are. This work bears supernatural fruit given by the Holy Spirit that appears in our natural world.

When we give to the needy, we are becoming the very feet, arms, and hands of God. We are showing His compassion and caring when we fulfill the needs of another person. John Ortberg, in his book, *The Life You've Always Wanted*, wisely asks this question and then provides his comment:

"Am I growing in love for God and people? The real issue is what kind of people we are becoming. Practices such as reading Scripture and praying are important—not because they prove how spiritual we are—but because God can use them to lead us into life."[9]

God knows what He has given to one hand, who in turn gives to the other hand that is able to give to the needy. Again, He gives us things so we can give to others and in this way, we become His hands and feet here on Earth.

Now the proper stage is set to talk about the specific steps to prayer. Jesus outlines them in the Lord's Prayer in both Matthew 6:9-13 and Luke 11:2-4. This would be a great way to start your journey of prayer. Although it really is so much more, I would love to share five simple principles that helped me immensely while I was trying to learn how to pray.

PRINCIPLE I:
"Our Father in heaven, hallowed be your name . . ."

This is a statement of worship. First and foremost, we need to learn to worship God. I used to start my prayers with my needs or centered around my desires. Although God knows our hearts and wants to hear from us, when we start our prayers focused on who He is and not on who we are, our prayers become more than just our needs. They become bigger, communal, and conversational. This time of worship, spent acknowledging who He is and what He can do, helps us to bridle our pride and ego. This allows us to humble ourselves and trust in whom we are coming to.

In the book of Job, God describes Himself to Job by asking him questions that shows His greatness. Here are just a few of those questions:

- "Where were you when I laid the earth's foundation?"
- "Have you ever given orders to the morning, or shown the dawn its place?"
- "Have the gates of death been shown to you?"
- "Have you comprehended the vast expanses of the earth?"

The questions go on, and it ends with this last question, kind of like, "here Job, can you do this? Cause I can."

"Can you raise your voice to the clouds and cover yourself with a flood of water? Do you send the lightning bolts on their way? Do they report to you, 'Here we are'?"

God isn't bragging. He has no need to do that. He is stating who He is and what He can do so we know in whose hands we are putting our lives.

Can anyone on this planet do any of the things God tells Job that He can? It's a comfort to know that who I am trusting can do unimaginable things. Yet, every day we put our faith in something far less capable. It is because of the greatness of God that we are assured that our prayers can be answered, plans can be made, and provisions met. Why not trust Him also to know a little better what is good for us? In the scope of a lifetime, He has much clearer vision. For the breadth of eternity, He has lived, created, loved, inspired, and planned.

Regarding the needs of our loved ones and even our enemies, how much more does He know about what they need? I don't believe we are worshipping God to elevate His ego, but rather to acknowledge Him in His glory so that we know who we are trusting. Oddly, the more time we spend in worship as we pray, the more confident we can become of our well-being, not because of who we are but because of who God is.

Although God may want to have an intimate and honest relationship with us, it is wise to remember to be reverent in attitude. The word "hallowed" means "set apart as holy."[10] God is our heavenly Father, creator of the heavens and earth,

Lord Almighty, the alpha and omega; not our biological father or a casual friend. This doesn't mean there is a requirement of using formal language when talking to Him, or acting properly (unless that suits you), rather it means having a humble and reverent attitude with an understanding of who you are conversing with.[11] An attitude of worship is an internal understanding of the character of God that can give us a righteous "reality check." Sometimes I worship by listening to music, by journaling, or by reading scripture such as the chapter of Job I referenced earlier. Almost always, worship includes an understanding and acknowledgment of the character of God. Remembering what He has already done, and attaching value to those actions, can help to remove pride from and establish trust in our hearts.

PRINCIPLE 2:
"Your kingdom come, your will be done on earth as it is in heaven . . . "

This principle is partly about a choice, a decision to choose God's kingdom and will for our lives. We acknowledge that His kingdom is coming; we are giving Him control and rule in our lives.

Kingdoms are ruled by authority. A good authority will use all its resources to protect, provide and care for everyone in its kingdom. This requires a choice based on trust. This is why it is helpful to start any conversation with God in worship.

I have read Job 38 many times to remind myself of the greatness of God and of His enormity and power. This is a king I trust to care for me, and this is the kingdom I want to be a part of. Spending time reading the Bible and learning about who God says He is and what He wants to give us makes our prayers so much more impactful. God is concerned with all of us under His protection. Parents who love all their children will not give one child under their care something they ask for if it will harm the family or be detrimental to any other child under their care. Neither will God.

Earlier I discussed the motives of our hearts and proposed that when we choose to put God *first* on our priority list we begin to step into His will, and He gives us the desires of our hearts. There are many unexpected cycles in God's principles.

One of them is that when we think of Him and of others, He takes care of us and our needs. He is about building up, not crushing. He is about loving others, not hating. He is about reconciliation, not crippling anger and bitterness. He is about community, not isolation and separation.

With all that was previously mentioned in mind, God doesn't give us everything we ask for. From His eternal perspective, He gives us what He knows is good for us. Are we concerned with earthly treasures or bringing God's kingdom here?

What is God's kingdom? *Guinness World Records* states that the Bible is the "best-selling book of non-fiction" selling over five billion copies worldwide.[12] It is this book that gives us a bit of a roadmap to finding our way around His kingdom. In this book, Jesus, who lives in community with God the Father, who stood by Him as our world was created, and who gave up so much to live with us; shows us how to be a leader by being a servant. It takes immense strength to serve as he did. It takes strength to give instead of receiving. It takes strength to be humble and meek. A life of humility and meekness is not built on weakness. It's a life built on strength often found because of prayer.

In Mark 14:36, Jesus' words reflect worship;

> *"Abba, Father," he said, "everything is possible for you. Take this cup from me. Yet not what I will, but what you will."*

Jesus is honest. He knows that what his Father is asking him to do will be unimaginably painful and tells his Father he would like another way out. Jesus doesn't spend time uttering a lengthy string of words. It's simple and intimate. He simply shares his heart, a heart I seek to emulate. Coming to God in prayer isn't about being a mindless robot or a doormat. It's about honesty and trust, revelation and choice.

God shines light and reveals things about His nature to us in prayer. He shares things about His kingdom here on Earth, things He would like done to save and redeem, to build and encourage. He gives us things so we can give to others (Proverbs 11:24-25). God isn't a hypocrite, and during his lifetime here on Earth,

Jesus modeled sincerity, truth, and honesty for us. He lived what he preached. He did not come, sit on a throne and order us around as servants. Jesus also doesn't ask us to do anything he didn't model for us, and does not ask us to do anything he does not equip us to do through him.

As Jesus awaited his persecution, he showed what was in his heart during this time with these simple words found in Luke 22:42, Mark 14:36, and Matthew 26:39: "But let your will be done rather than mine."

Although many of us face hardships, I don't think many of them compare to the hardship he knew he was about to face. Even worse than the physical pain he would endure while he was persecuted here on Earth in his natural body that felt every ounce of pain that each of our bodies do, it must have been absolute torture to carry all the sins of all humankind upon the holiest of backs. He would experience separation from God while he carried our sins straight into hell and left them with death. Not one of us here on this planet will escape without some sort of loss, loneliness, or separation from something we love. Neither did Jesus. He chose to experience all that he did so we could be with our Lord in eternity. Jesus wanted to accomplish the Father's will and to bring God's kingdom to us so much that he gave up everything to be with us. Would we give up everything and put God first? When we do, incredible things, extraordinary things, can happen because we begin to focus on Him and not ourselves.

When God gets involved in our lives, it invites supernatural interaction. It is then that we can see that He hears us and gives us what we ask for (Psalm 37:4-7). One of my favorite songs is by Lauren Daigle, *First*. The song gives perfect words to this thought of seeking God's will *first* in everything: "Before I bring my need, I will bring my heart/Before I lift my cares I will lift my arms/ . . . And seek You *first*."[13]

PRINCIPLE 3:
"Give us today our daily bread . . ."

This third principle models trust in God, a trust that must be renewed daily. "Give us what we need today," not "give me what I need for the next ten years, and I'll check back then with my next list." He wants to sit with us every day. How amazing is that? He wants to hear from us every moment of every day. We are that important to Him.

It is safe to say that all of our important relationships should be built around trust. He wants to know what we want. He wants to give us what nourishes us and what feeds us. This isn't always just our bodies but also our souls, and the intangibles such as our minds, emotions, and will. God is a supernatural being, so it doesn't surprise me that He is concerned with more than our natural and physical bodies. He wants more for us than to just meet our natural needs. He wants to multiply and make things supernatural for us. He wants to provide for us daily.

It is because of this principle that I have learned to ask God for what I would like but also for what He thinks is good for me. There are many times when I think of things to ask God for. There are things I think I desperately need but often ask that His will be done regardless of what I think I need. I cannot recall a single time that I was disappointed in what God has provided. It doesn't mean I have always received what I prayed for. It means that God's will has never disappointed me.

> *"Therefore do not worry about tomorrow, for tomorrow will worry about itself. Each day has enough trouble of its own"* (Matthew 6:34).

> *"Now listen, you who say, "Today or tomorrow we will go to this or that city, spend a year there, carry on business and make money." Why . . . you do not even know what will happen tomorrow. What is your life? . . . You are a mist that appears for a little while and then vanishes. Instead, you ought to say, "If it is the Lord's will, we will live and do this or that"* (James 4:13).

The Bible also says this about storing up things for yourself here on Earth by only being concerned with material possessions and tangible riches in Matthew 6:19-24:

We Have a Model: The Lord's Prayer

"Do not store up for yourselves treasures on earth, but store up for yourselves treasures in heaven. No one can serve two masters. Either you will hate the one and love the other, or you will be devoted to the one and despise the other. You cannot serve both God and money."

At the end of my trip to Russia, a tiny Russian lady came walking up to me, smiling. She handed me a tablecloth. It had stains on it, it was used, and the edges were a little ragged. Without an ounce of embarrassment, shame, or guilt, she looked straight into my eyes, grabbed my hands, and said something with an immense amount of confidence, gratefulness, and humility. It was short and yet so very profound: "I'm giving you what I can, but it is God who will give you what you need."

When I look at this tablecloth, I don't see those stains at all; I see the beautiful, faithful, grateful heart of this lady. She wanted to give me something to show her gratitude so she gave me what she had and knew in complete faith that God would give me what I needed.

Our list of needs is like that tablecloth—what we can imagine needing or wanting is nothing compared to what God can give us. We can give God our wish list, which to Him may look like a stained tablecloth. With humble hearts, sincere and honest conversation, we can offer them without embarrassment, shame, or guilt because they will be valued and treasured. But when we then set that tablecloth aside and let Him give us what He wants to give us, we can have so much more love, joy, and peace in our lives. He already knows what is in our hearts. What we are asking for won't surprise or overwhelm Him. Yet, if our lives are lived in God's will, focusing on bringing His kingdom here and what it represents, no matter where we are placed, we can give God what we can with our actions and ask Him to give us what we need to make them extraordinary.

PRINCIPLE 4:
"Forgive our debts, as we also have forgiven our debtors . . ."

This principle helps keep our hearts from pride, judgment, and lack of forgiveness. We confess our sins constantly and recognize that because God chooses to forgive us, we must also choose to forgive. A good place to look at God's heart on this is in Matthew 18:21-35, the *Parable of the Unmerciful Servant*. This parable is an answer Jesus gives to Peter when he asked this question:

> *"How many times shall I forgive my brother or sister who sins against me? Up to seven times?" Jesus answers, "I tell you, not seven times, but seventy-seven times."*

Jesus then shares this story:

> *"Therefore, the kingdom of heaven is like a king who wanted to settle accounts with his servants. As he began the settlement, a man who owed him ten thousand bags of gold was brought to him. Since he was not able to pay, the master ordered that he and his wife and his children and all that he had be sold to repay the debt. At this the servant fell on his knees before him. 'Be patient with me,' he begged, 'and I will pay back everything.' The servant's master took pity on him, canceled the debt, and let him go."*

In this parable, the amount that was owed was ten thousand talents, in Greek translation. This was a tremendous debt. Just one of those talents was worth about twenty years of a day laborer's wages or a total debt equivalent to several million dollars.[14] This was an amount that this servant couldn't possibly repay. This is vital to understanding that we all have debts that cannot possibly be paid back. It is also why the next part of this parable is so important. Our hearts are reflected in our actions. This servant was forgiven his debt and was let go.

However, when this same servant had the opportunity to extend the same kind of grace that was given to him, he chose to act quite differently:

> "But when that servant went out, he found one of his fellow servants who owed him a hundred silver coins. He grabbed him and began to choke him. 'Pay back what you owe me!' he demanded. His fellow servant fell to his knees and begged him, 'Be patient with me, and I will pay it back.' But he refused. Instead, he went off and had the man thrown into prison until he could pay the debt."

The amount owed in this situation was described as a few dollars.[15] This was a much smaller amount than what the first servant owed. This debt could reasonably be paid back. Yet right after his own unpayable debt had been canceled, this man chose to grab and choke his fellow servant and then put him in a situation that prevented him from repaying the much smaller debt. He had him thrown into debtor's prison. Yes, by law, he could do that. Yes, he was owed money. Yet, he chose *not* to extend the mercy, compassion, and freedom that he had just received. God has something very severe to say about this attitude in verses 31-35:

> "When the other servants saw what had happened, they were outraged and went and told their master everything that had happened. Then the master called the servant in. 'You wicked servant,' he said, 'I canceled all that debt of yours because you begged me to. Shouldn't you have had mercy on your fellow servant just as I had on you?' In anger his master handed him over to the jailers to be tortured, until he should pay back all he owed. This is how my heavenly Father will treat each of you unless you forgive your brother or sister from your heart."

God doesn't cancel our debts, so we can run around collecting from others without mercy and compassion. When we are treating others the way God treats us, our lives become extraordinary, and our efforts are multiplied and have supernatural influence because we are bringing God's kingdom here on Earth. Prayers get answered, and our souls are satisfied. If you want the beginnings of an extraordinary life, pray to be the person described in Colossians 3:12-15:

> "Therefore, as God's chosen people, holy and dearly loved, clothe yourselves with compassion, kindness, humility, gentleness, and patience. Bear with each other and forgive one another if any of you has a grievance against someone. Forgive as the Lord forgave you. And over all these virtues put on love, which binds them all together in perfect unity."

PRINCIPLE 5:
"And lead us not into temptation, but deliver us from the evil one . . ."

Before I went to Russia, there were many times I would forget this step when I prayed. I wasn't thinking of spiritual warfare. In James 4:7-8 it states:

"submit yourselves, then, to God. Resist the devil, and he will flee from you."

It's through our submission and closeness to God that Satan flees. It's not because of our own strength, courage, or actions. Satan isn't scared of us. It is God's power and rule that stop Satan. We resist him by being close to God and living according to His will. In Matthew 4:1-11, even Jesus was tempted by Satan. Jesus knows Satan misuses God's words and twists them to cause people to stumble. We often do this when we arm ourselves with the words we have memorized to condemn others. This is a large part of why I believe God's Word is the sword wielded by the Holy Spirit and used by us generally to build up, love, and encourage, but used by Him to convict and transform. It is in prayer that we use them, following the lead of the Holy Spirit for the glory of God, not to elevate ourselves into a position of judgment.

Jesus models the importance of understanding God's Word. His direct knowledge of scripture and reliance on truth revealed deception. He didn't act upon on Satan's persuasions, as Eve did in the Garden of Eden. The true power of resisting the devil comes in knowing God's Word for yourself. Don't rely on others to tell you what God says, investigate that for yourself. Memorize the words that are written and know their true context so that you can remain close to God and under His protection. As you read, pray for God's enlightenment and revelations through the Holy Spirit. I have been down many a lovely rabbit hole chasing the meaning of His Word. He loves revealing His truth to those who *ask* and *seek* and *knock*.

Here is the account of Jesus (in Matthew 4:1-10) being tested in the wilderness. It is a great example of how knowing God's word for ourselves saves us from Satan:

> *"Then Jesus was led by the Spirit into the wilderness to be tempted by the devil. After fasting forty days and forty nights, he was hungry. The tempter came to Him and said, "If you are the Son of God, tell these stones to become bread." Jesus answered, "It is written:*
>
> *'Man shall not live on bread alone, but on every word that comes from the mouth of God.'"*
>
> *Then the devil took Him to the holy city and had Him stand on the highest point of the temple.*
>
> *"If you are the Son of God," he said, "throw yourself down. For it is written: 'He will command his angels concerning you, and they will lift you up in their hands, so that you will not strike your foot against a stone.'" Jesus answered him, "It is also written: 'Do not put the Lord your God to the test.'" Again, the devil took Him to a very high mountain and showed Him all the kingdoms of the world and their splendor. "All this I will give you," he said, "if you will bow down and worship me." Jesus said to him, "Away from me, Satan! For it is written: 'Worship the Lord your God, and serve him only.'"*

The devil tempts us in order to lead us away from God. If he can inhibit our ability to love and reduce our ability to experience love, joy, peace, and a PKG of FiGS, our relationship with others and God will be greatly diminished. Satan can do this by encouraging us to elevate ourselves above God by being prideful, which leads to isolation, and selfishness. This is why I memorize scripture so that when I'm making decisions in my life, when I am tempted and when I am confused; I am protected. Being able to recite the appropriate verse gives me a peace of mind. They are not incantations; they are truth. It's with that sword that I can stand and cut the temptations that are laid before me. God will bring us through trials. Even so, He does not tempt us to break, humiliate, isolate, or otherwise harm ourselves. He allows trials so that we can grow and see Him, and also so that others can grow and see Him.

A simple way to decide if you are being tempted by Satan or in the midst of a trial that provides an opportunity for God to work in your life is to ask yourself, *who am I thinking of?* Will my actions and thoughts elevate me in anyway? Am I looking only to my own needs, ambitions, or satisfactions? Or, am I looking to God and what He wants? It sounds contradictory that when you want the best life and the best for yourself that you *wouldn't* look to fulfill your own needs.

This is another one of those unexpected cycles of God's economy: look to God's will, and you will be blessed in extraordinary ways. Satan is subtle and has had thousands of years to know how to push our buttons. If our thoughts and actions are prideful, then you can be assured, it's a temptation from Satan. Although God allows Satan to persuade, He does not give Satan complete freedom. There will be a day of payment and reconciliation; a balancing of the books for him, as well. Satan will be called to account. For now, God can use whatever footholds we have given Satan in our lives or anything thrown our way and turn it into good (Romans 8:28). He, Himself doesn't sling the mud, but He certainly can build something beautiful.

CHAPTER 10

ASK, SEEK, AND KNOCK

*"There are many ways of going forward,
but only one way of standing still."*
—Franklin D. Roosevelt

"I have been impressed with the urgency of doing. Knowing is not enough; we must apply. Being willing is not enough; we must do."
—Leonardo da Vinci

There are many examples of prayer in the Bible. Some are relatively simple, while other prayers are more complex. *The Lord's Prayer* is just one that we can learn from. While the Bible does not always tell us God's response to prayers, or give detailed information regarding specific and unique decisions that need to be made each day in our personal lives, it does tell us who God is and the type of relationship He wants to have with us. When we *ask*, *seek*, and *knock*, God does reveal our unique purpose which provides a frame for our lives.

Often our personal prayer life can feel not at all like a conversation. Conversations are meant to be two-sided, but often our prayers can feel one-sided.

We direct our thoughts, requests, and ideas to God. Then we end our prayers; done. Our conversation is over, and we don't know what God has or wants to say. We don't hear an audible voice, we don't have a face to look at, and no physical being is sitting in front of us staring back. Remember, though, that God has the universe at His disposal. He isn't limited to responding to each of us by sitting in a human physical form in front of us and only speaking words (Deuteronomy 5:24, Psalm 50:1, Daniel 2:28). On top of this, God has his own timing, one that is perfect and not ours (Ecclesiastes 3:1, 2 Peter 3:8), so an answer right away won't always be happening. He is weaving together many lives to bring us all into a perfect home when we are ready.

When we end our prayers, often we walk away before the best part of the conversation has happened. I am not talking about literally walking away. I'm talking about closing the conversation off in your mind. God knows our hearts, so He knows what we are going to say even before we begin to speak (Psalm 139:4).

What we often forget is that after we accept what Jesus has done for us and recognize who God is, the Holy Spirit is deposited in us. We, too, have a way to understand God through the Holy Spirit. The problem is, many times, we limit His communication to our own ideas and ways of thinking. We don't listen to or consider His ideas, thoughts, or requests. To want what God wants to give us is to, want more and not settle for less. What that less would be is whatever we come up with on our own. In this scenario, we also don't consider what we have already been given.

The richness of prayer comes in the in-between moments of asking, seeking, and knocking. Listening with an open mind helps us allow God to be a part of this conversation. I promise, He is not an empty echo of our thoughts. He can whisper or thunder (Job 37:5). He can speak anyway, anyhow, and to anyone He chooses.

Often He speaks to me in an urge, an idea, or a thought that seems out of character for me. He has reached me through dreams, through other people, and through situations. Many more times, He speaks with His own words through scripture I'm familiar with. When this happens, I find an opportunity to sit with

Him mentally even though I'm hardly ever in a quiet place when this happens. I often ask if there is something He would like me to do. It's a process of both patiently and persistently asking.

Many times, during prayer, I ask how I can help another person. One such time I had been praying for a woman whose husband left her with two small children. She was definitely dealing with some very real emotions and worries in her life. I was attending a large bible study at that time, and we broke off into smaller groups to discuss what we had learned. She was part of a small group with me for a session. I prayed for her and her two small ones in my quiet time for a couple of weeks but didn't feel that God had answered with any action I could take. One morning as I was running late, I had a strong urge to grab a large leather bracelet that had a silver plate attached that was engraved with scripture about God's love. In my mind, I questioned whether it was a frivolous desire. In that moment, it was a bracelet to finish off my outfit for the day, but today I felt a different sense of urgency when I put it on. Today I prayed it would be something He would use.

Later that morning, as I saw this woman among many other ladies in our group, I felt the need to take a few minutes during the lecture to write down a thought I had. It was a simple poem of sorts, but it was for her, letting her know that I had a garden she could sit in, a table to eat at, a place to breathe, if she needed. As we broke into our small groups, the urge became stronger and stronger that I needed to give her the bracelet and poem. I felt silly, asking God over and over if this is what He wanted, and if so, to please give me the opportunity to give it to her. Wouldn't you know, I was given a quiet moment with her and was able to give her those small gifts. I found out later that she was extremely encouraged by both items. The poem hung in a place of honor, her refrigerator, to remind her that God is working on her behalf and she will not be alone.

This is just a small example of how God is present in those small whispers, urges, and thoughts that call us to be bigger and better than ourselves. It is a difficult concept to grasp, how to listen to God, yet it seems so easy.

Right?

Wrong! I have talked with many women that feel like they are just talking in their heads when they are praying. They say that it feels like they are just listening to themselves. One particular verse catapulted me into a better understanding of how to hear God, but it took a lot of practice and time. It requires persistence with a mind focused on the character of God. Our minds must also be open to the things He chooses to do through us and in us. In hindsight, for many years, I was impatient, and my prayers reflected that. I believe now that the process of hearing God's voice and recognizing it took more time than I wanted because God was teaching me patience and perseverance!

> *"Ask and it will be given to you; seek and you will find; knock and the door will be opened to you. For everyone who asks receives; the one who seeks finds; and to the one who knocks, the door will be opened"* (Matthew 7:7-8).

In the previous chapter, in Matthew 6:16-24, (right after *The Lord's Prayer*), Jesus talks about "Fasting" and "Treasures in Heaven." Then in Matthew 6:25-34, he tells us "Do Not Worry." At the beginning of the next chapter (Matthew 7), Jesus talks about "not judging others," and *then* he talks about asking, seeking, and knocking. Each topic is mentioned in this order for a reason. There is a nugget of wisdom in each of them, and they are brilliantly pieced together like a roadmap for your journey of prayer.

FASTING

> *"When you fast, do not look somber as the hypocrites do, for they disfigure their faces to show others they are fasting. Truly I tell you, they have received their reward in full. But when you fast, put oil on your head and wash your face, so that it will not be obvious to others that*

you are fasting, but only to your Father, who is unseen; and your Father, who sees what is done in secret, will reward you" (Matthew 6:16-18).

Fasting encourages focus. When we are hungry, it takes discipline and self-control to pray. Fasting is sacrificial and brings our focus on God and not ourselves. People don't know you are choosing to give up something unless you tell them, and it requires personal sacrifice. We will be rewarded for focusing on something other than our immediate needs, and God sees our sacrifice.

TREASURES IN HEAVEN

"Do not store up for yourselves treasures on earth, where moths and vermin destroy, and where thieves break in and steal. But store up for yourselves treasures in heaven, where moths and vermin do not destroy, and where thieves do not break in and steal. For where your treasure is, there your heart will be also. The eye is the lamp of the body. If your eyes are healthy, your whole body will be full of light. But if your eyes are unhealthy, your whole body will be full of darkness. If then the light within you is darkness, how great is that darkness! No one can serve two masters. Either you will hate the one and love the other, or you will be devoted to the one and despise the other. You cannot serve both God and money" (Matthew 6:19-24).

Jesus urges us to have priorities that line up with God's. This verse refers to true treasure, a treasure that can be received when we live a sacrificial life and become committed to God. He knows what we do in secret. He knows the most secret of desires, the ones that hide deep in our hearts. He knows them all, good and bad, and still urges us to want what He has to offer; things no one can steal from us. If we *only* focus or if *all* our thoughts are on only earthly treasures, we miss out on the true wealth. We miss out on answered prayers. We miss out on the things God wants to give us.

DO NOT WORRY

> "Therefore I tell you, do not worry about your life, what you will eat or drink; or about your body, what you will wear. Is not life more than food, and the body more than clothes? Look at the birds of the air; they do not sow or reap or store away in barns, and yet your heavenly Father feeds them. Are you not much more valuable than they? Can any one of you by worrying add a single hour to your life? And why do you worry about clothes? See how the flowers of the field grow. They do not labor or spin.
>
> Yet I tell you that not even Solomon in all his splendor was dressed like one of these. If that is how God clothes the grass of the field, which is here today and tomorrow is thrown into the fire, will He not much more clothe you—you of little faith? So do not worry, saying, 'What shall we eat?' or 'What shall we drink?' or 'What shall we wear?' For the pagans run after all these things, and your heavenly Father knows that you need them. But seek first His kingdom and His righteousness, and all these things will be given to you as well. Therefore do not worry about tomorrow, for tomorrow will worry about itself. Each day has enough trouble of its own" (Matthew 6:25-34).

Even after telling us what we should be concerned with, Jesus knows we will still worry. God wants our lives to reflect His influence in them. We, ourselves, are not supernatural so this verse tells us how much God cares for us and is willing to give us to meet our earthly needs and even more. We don't have to spend every minute of the day consumed with meeting those needs or spend every minute of our prayers relaying these needs. We can do that but it doesn't bear much fruit, and it doesn't effectively bring God into the conversation in the way He would like to show Himself. God wants to say and give us so much more than we can imagine.

JUDGING OTHERS

> *"Do not judge, or you too will be judged. For in the same way you judge others, you will be judged, and with the measure you use, it will be measured to you. Why do you look at the speck of sawdust in your brother's eye and pay no attention to the plank in your own eye? How can you say to your brother, 'Let me take the speck out of your eye,' when all the time there is a plank in your own eye? You hypocrite, first take the plank out of your own eye, and then you will see clearly to remove the speck from your brother's eye"* (Matthew 7:1-5).

This last verse before Jesus tells us to *"ask, seek, and knock"* is another favorite of mine. It taught me to choose mercy. It taught me to ask, "what is my part in this situation or what can I do to help?" rather than blaming others for what they are or are not doing. We are asked not to judge others, or we too will be judged in the same manner.

Being truthful and honest are very good attributes, but we all make mistakes. Therefore it is good to have mercy, compassion, and understanding because God extends mercy to us. If admitting our own faults (the specks in our own eye) requires a relationship with God and help of the Holy Spirit, how much more do we need to exhibit that same level of compassion when helping someone else? How can we judge someone else's heart when we have not lived their life? This doesn't mean not to be truthful or honest about what offends; it means extending compassion and mercy. After all, we ask God to do that with us all the time. We may have a long list of offenses, but our prayers will be more fruitful if they are grounded in mercy and compassion rather than retribution and revenge.

Jesus gives us some instruction, models prayer for us, and then gives us some boundaries for our minds and hearts. He wants us to focus on Him (which may require personal sacrifice), look for the treasures that are eternal, not worry about our daily needs every minute of the day, and not judge others. With all these previous verses in mind, now we can ask and be confident that God will answer.

FINALLY: ASK, SEEK, KNOCK

> *"Ask and it will be given to you; seek and you will find; knock and the door will be opened to you.*
> *For everyone who asks receives; the one who seeks finds; and to the one who knocks, the door will be opened"* (Matthew 7:7-8).

ASK

Many people take this verse out of context and think that they can ask for anything and God will give it to them. Then in their disappointment, they can walk away from prayers or feel empty and unfulfilled. This verse is not meant to entitle us to whatever we ask for. In context, it follows verses that remind us that God is concerned with our sacrificial focus and the treasures we pursue. We are assured that God knows our most essential needs and doesn't want us to worry that He won't take care of them. He wants more for us than just the bare necessities.

In God's economy, we are given so that we can give. In so doing people are cared for. Judging others or withholding compassion and mercy from them will not be honored by God. We are asked to love our enemy. Yet, loving our enemy or not judging another does not require us to be doormats. Right after Jesus tells us not to judge others, he says to deal with your own issues, faults, or wrong behavior before you straighten out your neighbor. Then he says these few, but important words in Matthew 7:6:

> *"Do not give dogs what is sacred; do not throw your pearls to pigs. If you do, they may trample them under their feet, and turn and tear you to pieces."*

Ask, Seek, and Knock

There is a difference between judgment and discernment. Judgment and lack of forgiveness can allow seeds of bitterness, anger, and resentment to grow. These things separate us from God. Having discernment in knowing that certain situations or relationships are unhealthy is a different matter. There are times when it is appropriate to just walk (or run) away (Proverbs 4:14-15, Matthew 10:23). When we ask God for things, we must know that He wants to give us good things and not things to harm us or others (Matthew 7:9-12).

It is easy to imagine asking. It is a natural beginning to most of our prayers and most of our conversations. It's a process that I don't need to spend much time on because it's natural to us. Perhaps that's why God asks us to start there, with something every single person on this planet can do. Even babies begin most of their conversations by asking, and no one teaches that. We ask. But it's just the beginning. In terms of your prayer life, this is just the beginning, as well. When I first started praying regularly, I just asked for things for myself and loved ones. I just asked. Scripture doesn't contradict itself, but it can make refinements. In Matthew, it simply says *"ask and it will be given,"* but there is more to follow in that statement; *"seek and you will find."* In the seeking of God and His character, you will find the refinements to this in verses such as:

> *"This is the confidence we have in approaching God: that if we ask anything according to His will, He hears us"* (1 John 5:14).

> *"And when you do ask, you do not receive, because you ask with wrong motives, that you may squander it on your pleasures"* (James 4:3).

A very popular verse in the Christian culture comes from Jeremiah 29:11:

> *"For I know the plans I have for you,"* declares the Lord, *"plans to prosper you and not to harm you, plans to give you hope and a future."*

You can see these words on many a trinket and t-shirt, but what follows is equally important and confirms what is said in Matthew. God does want us to ask and to prosper, but He says:

> *"Then you will call on me and come and pray to me, and I will listen to you. You will seek me and find me when you seek me with all your heart. I will be found by you," declares the Lord, "and will bring you back from captivity"* (Jeremiah 29:12-14).

God has a plan, and it includes good things for us. When we call on Him in prayer, we are promised that He will listen. After we call and pray then we must actively seek. If we seek God with all our hearts, He will be found, and we will be brought out of captivity.

The prophet Jeremiah was relaying God's words to a specific group of exiled people. In our own lives, we all are held captive by something. So if you are asking for something, please don't stop. Once you are finished with that step, you are ready to start seeking. This movement is filled with purpose and intent. It's filled with an investigative will, a desire to uncover something, and a questioning nature. If you have made the choice to move towards God, then let your prayers reflect that movement by seeking Him and His will for your life. Let your asking evolve into a persistent investigative movement towards Him.

SEEK

If we are told "to seek" and it is not in plain sight, then we may need help. 1 Corinthians 2:7 states:

> *". . . we declare God's wisdom, a mystery that has been hidden and that God destined for our glory before time began."*

The reason it is not in plain sight isn't that it's not there; we just cannot see it. Many parents who celebrate Easter understand this intuitively. We hide treasures, whether its candy, eggs, toys, or baskets filled with goodies. The point isn't to keep the treasure from those we care for; it's to allow them to search. We want good things for them, and we want to see joy on their faces when they find it. Like God, we walk alongside our children. If needed, we give them hints. When they look to us, we reveal what we had hidden earlier. It is their choice to follow our directions and gather their reward. Sure, we can run around with them and gather all the treasure for them, but how does that help them grow and discover?

As they grow, we don't need to reveal the easy stuff anymore. We may not walk holding their hands, but we keep an eye out waiting for their invitation and questions. Perhaps, in their excitement, they run too fast, or they are distracted looking at others in pursuit of their treasure, or they don't see the obstacles in front of them because they are worried about the treasure that is further away. We watch, and although we are ready to help, we are hoping they will get back up and continue their search. When they don't, or can't, as loving parents, we help them up and urge them forward to continue their search, knowing that it will be worth the effort. As our children age, the hiding spots get more challenging. With time, the pursuit has to become their own.

More years pass, and if you've seen the difference between young grade-school children and older high school children at an egg hunt, you will understand; as they have aged life gets more complicated. Their interests expand and their enthusiasm wanes. They start becoming distracted by other things as they begin to become more aware. In a very simplified way, it's a little like when Adam and Eve ate from the Tree of Knowledge of good and evil and discovered they felt ashamed because of their nakedness. They hid from God and tried to hide themselves; they were not as free.

The same thing can happen to our children and to us. As we explore the world, we can lose sight of who God created us to be and what He thinks of us. If we stop looking for our identity through God and His Word, we are in danger of letting people in this world or even ourselves choose our treasure. I guarantee the treasure that you and I can dream up can in no way compare to the treasure God can dream up.

As we mature, things do change. Good was what God planned for us; a fulfilling relationship with Him. We can choose to live in a *spiritual* Garden of Eden by seeking God constantly. Wherever God is, there Eden will be for us. We just need to invite Him to where we are, and He brings His kingdom to us with His presence. For example, we have a choice to ask for material things here on earth, which is not a bad thing, but if our desire for that thing becomes more important than God, then it becomes an idol. If our security and well-being are placed in something other than God then what we are asking for is contrary to what He wants for us, and we begin to worship a false idol. We are created for worship, but not to worship the things of this world.

Like generations of parents before us, we want our children to mature and find true love and happiness. We want them to move towards building a good life for themselves. We no longer hold their hands every step of the way. It is a natural cycle of life. We want good things for them, often at our own expense. Wouldn't many honorable men and women give their lives to give good things to the ones they love?

As we grow older, we may begin to realize that a meaningful life will require aspirations towards something more than merely fulfilling our own needs and desires. We develop friendships that make our world bigger. Some people have children, which is a decision that often changes the focus of their lives. The relationships that cause us to think more of others out of love and less of ourselves is similar to our relationship with God. As we mature, most seek to make their world bigger. Possibly, it is an innate need so that we also find out that we need God. We need something divine that is bigger than ourselves. When we fall, we can trust that there is no limit to the breadth and width of our safety net. Perhaps we were wired that way by a God we can never outgrow. This is why He assures us repeatedly that if we seek Him, He will reveal Himself to us. It's good to hunt, and it's ok to fall because if we are focused on God, then we know we are safe. When we do, we find that God is so much more than a safety net. Even the most intellectual of seekers will never outgrow Him.

It is natural that as we mature in our relationship with our Maker, our questions change. Life changes and so do our responses and concerns and priorities. Regardless of how those treasure hunts continue, we are held accountable for what God has revealed to us and for what we pass on to others:

> "Not many of you should become teachers, my fellow believers, because you know that we who teach will be judged more strictly" (James 3:1).

It's not that God doesn't want us to teach. I believe God does not want us to pass on nor accept counterfeit treasure. The best way to do this is to always spend time investigating and seeking God personally. As we grow spiritually and as our roles change, we become more like the older children in the egg hunt, the ones willing to help the younger ones.

For many years I read my Bible and didn't have passion or excitement about it, but I did it because it was the right thing to do. Prayer changed that for me. I started inviting God, through the Holy Spirit, to translate for me, to reveal things to me. I wanted Him to make the words on the page living. I prayed that those words would become personal to me and reveal what God wanted me to find that day. It's wonderful knowing God's truth, but it's extraordinary and powerful when it becomes personal and revealed through His involvement. God speaks to us supernaturally when we invite Him to join us when we are seeking Him.

KNOCK

Knocking requires intention, repetition, and persistence. It is an action. In John14:23, Jesus says:

> "Anyone who loves me will obey my teaching. My Father will love them, and we will come to them and make our home with them."

COME FILL THIS PLACE

In this passage, Jesus gives an invitation to a home that he and his father have made. It's built on love and obedience, and it requires change and growth. Many of the homes we seek to build with our own families here on Earth are built on this same premise. Whereas seeking is an attempt to find something, knocking implies that we have found it and are actively trying to get to it. This isn't about knocking all over town, trying out different houses and moving on when our needs aren't met. It is an action that requires a commitment to stand in a chosen place and ask for entrance. We know what is on the other side because we have looked for it.

God doesn't force our submission. He doesn't try to force us into a relationship with Him. Instead, He waits, until we know what He has done for us through His son and we ask for an invitation into His kingdom. He wants us to come willingly with our eyes wide open. For many of us, we knock because we want something better. God has designed many things improve our lives. His plans have been laid out before any of us were born.

> "But the plans of the Lord stand firm forever, the purposes of His heart through all generations" (Psalm 33:11).

> "For everyone who asks receives; the one who seeks finds; and to the one who knocks, the door will be opened. This is a promise from the same God who laid out the "purposes of his heart through all generations" (Matthew 7:8).

We have already seen scripture that outlines God's character. He doesn't change His mind, and He doesn't break promises. If your prayers seem empty and isolated, stand at the door and keep knocking as loud as you can. God will give you entrance. You may have to be patient, but be confident that your prayers matter, and God hears them.

I previously shared that I lived a very reckless and challenging life in my late teens. I made bad decisions, got pregnant and had an abortion. Those actions carved a giant hole in my heart that I tried to fill in a dance club. Another girl who I had often seen there had also gotten pregnant, and I found out later that she had kept her baby. Years went by, and as I grew in my faith, she would often come to my mind. I asked God to bless her for making a decision not to abort. I prayed that God would bless her for choosing something that did not require an innocent life to be given up. I prayed for her child, hoping God had His hand in its life and that He had provided for them. For close to eighteen years I prayed for them, not knowing how their lives turned out.

For some of our prayers, we don't get to know how God answers, but in this case, I found her sitting next to me in a Bible study almost two decades later. I was speechless, and it took a couple of weeks before I could share with her that I had been praying for her and her child. She shared that her daughter was a missionary in another country and although she went through difficult times, she felt God's presence in her life. At the time that we spoke, it was clear from the evidence of her life that she loved God and He had blessed her and her child.

My prayers weren't the only reason she was blessed, but it was amazing to know that they helped to contribute to her well-being. I share this because it taught me never to stop praying. People, events, and thoughts often pop into my head. I don't know the circumstances surrounding their lives, but I believe prayer can be a formidable weapon that can be used as an intercession for those in need. The Holy Spirit does understand what is happening and through Him, we are able to fight these spiritual battles.

My in-laws prayed for me since I was a little child. They didn't know who they were praying for, as they were praying for my husband's future spouse. I was lavished with prayers even before I called to God or recognized Him for who He was. They were praying for me during the difficult times in my life, like when I was trying to commit suicide. They were praying for me while I was struggling to make a life worth living, they were praying for me as I grew, and they continue to pray for me even now. They may not have been praying in the exact moments that I experienced specific things, but they blanketed my life in prayer, and since God is timeless, I believe those prayers mattered immensely. I know to me, they are invaluable. I believe those prayers helped me find my way to them, to stand in their kitchen and make a decision that transformed me.

It's like the question, which came first, the chicken or the egg? Does the person or situation that we feel a need to pray for come from our own thoughts or does God place that person or situation in our thoughts? God is timeless and is always working on our behalf, even before we know who He is. God hears us and if you don't see the answers to your prayers, be assured that they do matter and God hears them. If you need to stand at that door and knock for eighteen years or more, then knock as loud as you can and don't ever give up. Your prayers are valuable, no matter who they are for.

> *"Which of you, if your son asks for bread, will give him a stone? Or if he asks for a fish, will give him a snake? If you, then, though you are evil, know how to give good gifts to your children, how much more will your Father in heaven give good gifts to those who ask him!"* (Matthew 7:9-11).

In other words, if we, being made in the image of God, can give good gifts and want to give good things to those we love, how much more can God give and how much more does He want to give good things to us? After all, He created the heavens and earth out of nothing. What has any one of us created out of nothing? His gifts are, literally, not of this world. Our knocking will not be wasted. The question is, do we want what God wants to give us and are we willing to knock until He gives it to us? If He doesn't give us what we ask for, do we choose to trust that He knows what is best for us and take what He offers? Do we choose to believe what He promises in the Bible to be real? Knowing what God wants to give us will change our lives and our hearts.

In relation to your prayer life, don't ever stop pursuing God; He wants to be found. Remember, in Jeremiah 29:13, God says: *"You will seek me and find me when you seek me with all your heart."* It doesn't say, "when you seek me with perfect wisdom, perfect words, or perfect prayers or with a perfect life;" it says, *"You will find me when you seek me with all your heart."*

A very close friend of mine lost her thirty-two-year-old son. His four-year-old son and two-year-old daughter have been left fatherless. She and her husband will have to find a way to continue their lives without their treasured child. My friend has always been gifted with the ability to love. I have encountered very few during my lifetime that can love like her. As she walked through her grief, she shared that she didn't feel close to God. She couldn't connect. I have felt this way at times, and I imagine many other people feel this way for one reason or another. Even in the midst of feeling unconnected, my friend pressed on. Just days after her son passed, her prayer was a simple plea that God let her know her son was with Him. In a very personal and unorthodox way, God did that for her. During an extremely difficult and challenging time, she was able to experience God's peace and joy for a short respite as she knew He had answered her prayer.

In another instance, what helped her was a devotional, one which stood out because it had been given to her by two different people at two different times in her life. Ten years earlier, after my friend lost her mother, she received a devotional from her sister-in-law. After losing her son, my friend received the same devotional from her niece. As she read the words when she opened the devotional after her son died, they spoke intimately and personally to her heart and situation. She felt the connection again. God can use anything to speak to us, especially His Word.

I, too, had a conversation with God about my friend and He gave me a picture of His plan and intent for her heart. As I said, my friend has a God-given gift to love in an extraordinary capacity. As I sat in prayer over her situation, I pleaded that God take away her pain. What I saw was a biological heart, full and soft and beating with strength. As I continued my conversation with God, the picture in my head changed; I could see stark branches without life wrapping around this beautiful heart and trapping it in a cage. The conversation continued, mostly with me asking God to take her pain away. I clearly heard the answer, "no." Many times I wrestle with God, and I never win, so I don't know why I do, but in this case, I continued to ask. The next picture I saw was that same heart with the same lifeless branches wrapped around it, except now a garden of greenery sprouted from underneath those branches, surrounding them and the heart. The greenery flourished until I could no longer see the heart or the dead branches. I realized that God would not take the pain away immediately, but I knew that her joy would flourish again. Days later, as we sat over coffee, she told me of the things happening in her life, and although she still suffers, I do see those sprigs of greenery sprouting. There are many ways God wants to connect, and He speaks to each of us uniquely and personally. God wants that connection, and I promise, the ONLY way that it doesn't happen is if you don't try.

He doesn't expect us to do all the work. God, too, stands at our door and knocks. He is close, not far away in the spiritually unattainable realms of mystery and divinity. He is here at our door, already, waiting to be invited in:

> *"Here I am! I stand at the door and knock. If anyone hears my voice and opens the door, I will come in and eat with that person, and they with me"* (Revelation 3:20).

I would love to walk alongside you and hear of your journey. Everyone has a story that needs to be told and can live a life worth living. If it doesn't feel like that now, then ask, seek, and knock until that changes. Invite God in with confidence, knowing that He is standing just on the other side of a door that you have the power to open. Our journey is never finished; it just continues from a different venue.

There are so many things to explore with God, and I look forward to growing old with Him in my heart and by my side. Pray with everything you have, for as much time as it takes, and embrace the journey. I have been praying for you and perhaps while in eternity, we will have a conversation over that cup of coffee.

Ask, Seek, and Knock

"My powers are ordinary. Only my application brings me success."
—Isaac Newton

"Don't Stop Believin'"
—Journey

ACKNOWLEDGMENTS

Many people have challenged, taught, encouraged, inspired and loved me in my life. They all have a part in this book; I'm sorry I cannot mention everyone by name.

I want to first thank my wonderful husband, Dave, who loves me every day, for better or worse. He begins his day much earlier than me but always makes sure that when I wake up, there is a cup of coffee next to me on my dresser. He has patiently listened to all my ideas, rough drafts and did my first endless round of edits. This book would not have happened without him.

My three shining stars and wonderful princesses, Chelsie, Elyssa, and Torrie inspire me to be the best mother I can be, and I thank God for them every day. They have filled my life with love, and they are a big part of the reason I began this journey in prayer. I thank them for those wonderful conversations in the car while having our "seat belt" time that drove me to serious conversations with God.

Thank you to my twin sister Darlene Alliston who has literally been there from the beginning. She has taught me how to celebrate each victory no matter how small it may seem to others. Sometimes getting out of bed in the morning is the victory.

Many family members supported me in writing this book. My Father and Mother-in-law, John and Jane Dietz, modeled the type of Christian living that changed the trajectory of my life. They prayed for me for most of my life, even before they even knew me. I treasure my "family" time with the Dietz, Stupar, Chin, Gutierrez, Sanchez, Avarca, Alliston, Gizzi, Hesselgrave, Stiger, Frothinger, and Hilby clans, who remind me that we are each unique and valuable.

COME FILL THIS PLACE

Special thanks to my Uncle George Antonio who answered the phone very late one night and reminded me why I'm writing this book.

To my friend Susie Ingold - I love you and thank you for being the leader of women and listener of God that you are. You have been a wonderful encouragement all these years.

Rhonda and John Pieracci, thank you for sharing your love with my family all these years. I pray that your story and Ryan's story will make a difference to others; inspiring them to heal from their pain. Hopefully they will choose to look to God when they search for a way to continue after such a tragedy. Rhonda, you love like no other.

My sunshine friend, Jeanine McKelvey, thank you for trying to rescue this stray. Thank you for inspiring me to enjoy people and challenging me to reach out into the world with your example.

Greg Kelner, thank you for driving from Santa Barbara so long ago to check on me. God saved me that day through you. Many times, I am reminded that God uses the most unaware to show His love to the most desperate. You were unaware of my desperation, but God spoke to me through your act of love. Thank you.

Thank you, Juan, for using your talent and skill in areas of design and photography to make me and this book look pretty! Steve, thank you for the edits and thoughtful contributions you gave which provided clarity and accuracy when needed.

Thank you, Willa Robinson, for answering a text from a stranger and meeting me in the coffee shop. I knew as soon as our first conversation that you would be an amazing publisher. Can you adopt me too?

NOTES

CHAPTER 1

1. Exodus verse 36. (n.d.). In *Pulpit Commentary*. Retrieved from https://biblehub.com/exodus/12-36.htm.
2. Sadducee Jewish Sect. (n.d.). In A. Augustyn, P. Bauer, B. Duignan, A. Eldridge, E. Gregersen, J. Leubering, . . . A. Zelazko (Ed.), *In Enclyopaedia Britannica*. Retrieved from https://www.britannica.com/topic/Sadducee.
3. The Scribes—Jewish leaders in the New Testament. (n.d.) Retrieved from https://www.bible-history.com/Scribes/THE_SCRIBESTeachers.htm

CHAPTER 2

1. Pride. (2018). In *Merriam-Webster.com*. Retrieved from https://www.merriam-webster.com/dictionary/pride.
2. Humble. (2018). In *Merriam-Webster.com*. Retrieved from https://www.merriam-webster.com/dictionary/humble.
3. Rice, J. (2014). The Incommunicable Attributes of God. Retrieved from https://intervarsity.org/blog/incommunicable-attributes-god.
4. *What are the attributes of God?* (2018). Retrieved from https://www.gotquestions.org/attributes-God.html. Recommended resource: *Knowing God* by J.I. Packer.
5. God: The attributes of God. (2018). Retrieved from https://www.blueletterbible.org/faq/attributes.cfm.

6. Quest Bible. [Kindle]. Retrieved from Philippians 2, Imitating Christ's, Humility, paragraph 1.
7. *What is the meaning of perfection in the Bible?* (n.d.). Retrieved from https://www.gotquestions.org/perfection-in-the-Bible.html. Recommended resource: *Balancing the Christian Life* by Charles Ryrie.
8. Bohlinger, T. (2018, September 26). *Kierkegaard's leap of faith.* [The Logos Academic blog]. Retrieved from https://academic.logos.com/kierkegaards-leap-of-faith/.
9. Moreland, J. P., & Craig, W. L. (2017). *Philosophical foundations for a Christian worldview* (2nd ed.). Downers Grove, IL: IVP Academic.
10. Piper, J. (2015). *A Godward life: Seeing the supremacy of God in all of life*. Colorado Springs, CO: Multnomah Books.
11. Jacobson, R. A. (2013). Moses, the golden calf, and the false images of the true god [Abstract]. *Word and World*.
12. Stewart, D. (n.d.) *What caused Satan's fall?* Blue Letter Bible [US]. Retrieved from https://www.blueletterbible.org/faq/don_stewart/don_stewart_75.cfm.

CHAPTER 3
1. Crown Financial Ministries. (2006). Biblical financial study.

CHAPTER 4
1. Word counts: How many times does a word appear in the Bible? (n.d.). Retrieved from https://www.christianbiblereference.org/faq_WordCount.htm.
2. Selfishness. (2018). In *Merriam-Webster.com*. Retrieved from https://www.merriam-webster.com/dictionary/selfishness.
3. Spurgeon, C. H. (1873, August 31). The Heart of Flesh [Sermon #1129]. *Metropolitan Tabernacle Pulpit*. Retrieved from https://www.spurgeongems.org/vols19-21/chs1129.pdf.

4. Spurgeon, C. H. (1862, May 25). The stony heart removed.[Sermon 456] *Metropolitan Tabernacle Pulpit*. Retrieved from https://www.spurgeon.org/resource-library/sermons/the-stony-heart-removed#flipbook/.
5. Spurgeon, C. H. (1862, May 25). The stony heart removed.[Sermon 456] *Metropolitan Tabernacle Pulpit*. Retrieved from https://www.spurgeon.org/resource-library/sermons/the-stony-heart-removed#flipbook/.
6. Bevere, J. (2011). The Bait of Satan. [Kindle]. Devotional Supplement, Day 9, paragraph 2.
7. Fried, L.S. (2003, October). Cyrus the Messiah. *The BAS Library*. Retrieved from https://www.baslibrary.org/bible-review/19/5/3.
8. King Cyrus of Persia. (2013). Retrieved from http://www.biblehistory.net/newsletter/cyrus.htm.
9. Stewart, D. (n.d.) Why did Jesus speak in Parables? Retrieved from https://www.blueletterbible.org/faq/don_stewart/don_stewart_1345.cfm.
10. Encyclopaedia Britannica Editors. (n.d.). Hide-and-seek. In *Encyclopaedia Britannica*. Retrieved from https://www.britannica.com/topic/hide-and-seek-game.

CHAPTER 5
1. Yaro, J.J. (n.d.). Intercession "Standing in the gap"? What does that mean. Retrieved from https://independent.academia.edu/JerryJYaro.

CHAPTER 6
1. Craig, W. L. (2003). *Hard Questions, Real Answers*. Wheaton, IL: Crossway Books. p 35.

CHAPTER 7
1. Zuch, R. B., Merrill, E., Constable, T., Heater, Jr., H., & Chisholm, Jr., R. (1991). *A Biblical Theology of the Old Testament*. Chicago, IL: Moody Press.

2. Fowler, L. (2011). Freedom in Christ. *Focus on the Family.* Retrieved from https://www.focusonthefamily.com/parenting/ spiritual-growth-for-kids/freedom-in-christ.
3. Lewis, C. S. (1943). *The Screwtape letters.* New York: Macmillan Co.
4. Does God Love Satan? - Gotquestions.org. (n.d.). Retrieved from https://www.gotquestions.org/does-God-love-Satan.html.
5. Zuch, R. B., Merrill, E., Constable, T., Heater, Jr., H., & Chisholm, Jr., R. (1991). *A Biblical Theology of the Old Testament.* Chicago, IL: Moody Press. p. 18.
6. History.com editors. (2018, February 2). Ephesus. Retrieved from https://www.history.com/topics/ancient-greece/Ephesus. Chapter 4.
7. Zondervan NIV Study Bible. *Introduction to book of Ephesians.*
8. Full Amor of God. (n.d.). Retrieved from http://www.christianarsenal.com/Christian_Arsenal/Full_Armor_of_God.html,
9. Ibid.
10. Fowler, L. (2011). Freedom in Christ. *Focus on the Family.* Retrieved from https://www.focusonthefamily.com/ parenting/ spiritual-growth-for-kids/freedom-in-christ.
11. Full Amor of God. (n.d.). Retrieved from http://www.christianarsenal.com/Christian_Arsenal/Full_Armor_of_God.html.
12. Ibid.
13. Ibid.
14. Thorn, J. (2017, May 29). Don't pursue feelings. Pursue Christ. *Ligonier Ministries.* Retrieved from https://www.ligonier.org/blog/ dont-pursue-feelings-pursue-christ/.
15. Full Amor of God. (n.d.). Retrieved from http://www.christianarsenal.com/Christian_Arsenal/Full_Armor_of_God.htmlc.

Notes

CHAPTER 8

1. *One In Three and Three in One* | Grace Communion International. (n.d.) Retrieved from https://www.gci.org/articles/one-in-three-and-three-in-one/.
2. Can you explain the Trinity? Retrieved from everystudent.com.
3. Ibid.
4. Power. (2018). In *Merriam-Webster.com*. Retrieved from https://www.merriam-webster.com/dictionary/power.
5. Seal. (2018). 2018). In *Merriam-Webster.com*. Retrieved from https://www.merriam-webster.com/dictionary/seal.
6. Mullen, B. A. (1996). Dictionaries – Baker's evangelical dictionary of Biblical theology—Seal. Retrieved from https:// www.biblestudytools.com/dictionary/seal/.
7. *Ancient Seals and Signets (Bible History Online)*. (n.d.). Retrieved from https://www.bible-history.com/sketches/ancient/seals.html.
8. Ibid.

CHAPTER 9

1. *How many times is "prayer" mentioned in the Bible?* Reference. Retrieved from https://www.reference.com/world-view/many-times-prayer-mentioned-bible-3a64e852ee9a3ca7.
2. Yawn, B. (n.d.). *Bible Study Tools.com: What is the significance of the Beatitudes?* [Video file]. Retrieved from https://www. godtube.com/watch/?v=WLKLWWNX.
3. Ibid.
4. Pure. (2018). In *Merriam-Webster.com*. Retrieved from https://www.merriam-webster.com/dictionary/pure.
5. Jones, R. (2011, April 27). *The Lord's Prayer in Hawaiian*. 2:10 [Video file]. Retrieved from https://www.youtube.com/watch?v=2UA3TbqI4Mg.

6. Farley, H. (2016, March 23). *What's the most common word in Scripture?* Christian Today. Retrieved from https://www.christiantoday.com/article/whats-the-most-common-word-in-scripture-five-facts-you-might-not-know-about-the-bible/82535.htm.
7. *Popular Bible Words.* The King James Bible Online. Retrieved from https://www.kingjamesbibleonline.org/Popular-Bible-Words.php.
8. Ibid.
9. Ortberg, J. (2002). *The life you've always wanted.* Grand Rapids, MI: Zondervan. p. 39.
10. *What does it mean to have reverence for God?* Retrieved from https://www.gotquestions.org/reverence-for-God.html.
    Recommended Resource: *Thinking. Loving. Doing. A Call to Glorify God with Heart and Mind* by John Piper & David Mathis.
11. Piper, J. (2016, April 29). What is Worship? [Audio transcript]. Retrieved from https://www.desiringgod.org/interviews/what-is-worship.
12. *Best-selling book of non-fiction.* Guinness World Records Limited 2019. Retrieved from http://www.guinnessworldrecords.com/world-records/best-selling-book-of-non-fiction.
13. Daigle, L. (2015, April 15). *Lauren Daigle—First* (Lyric Video). [Video file]. Retrieved from https://www.youtube.com/watch?v=RbWQV3OiRqA
14. Massay, P. (2010, October 27). *The parable of the two debtors in modern terms.* The Biola University Chimes. Retrieved from https://chimesnewspaper.com/13189/opinions/parable-two-debtors/.
15. Ibid.

APPENDIX

SCRIPTURE REFERENCES

DEDICATION

Genesis 1:27 So God created mankind in his own image, in the image of God he created them; male and female he created them.

Isaiah 61:1-3 The Spirit of the Lord God is upon me, because the Lord has anointed me to bring good news to the afflicted; He has sent me to bind up the brokenhearted, to proclaim liberty to captives and freedom to prisoners; to proclaim the favorable year of the Lord and the day of vengeance of our God; to comfort all who mourn, to grant those who mourn in Zion, giving them a garland instead of ashes, the oil of gladness instead of mourning, the mantle of praise instead of a spirit of fainting. So they will be called oaks of righteousness, the planting of the Lord, that He may be glorified.

John 15:9 As the Father has loved me, so have I loved you. Now remain in my love.

John 14:26 But the Advocate, the Holy Spirit, whom the Father will send in my name, will teach you all things and will remind you of everything I have said to you.

INTRODUCTION

Romans 8:16 The Spirit himself testifies with our spirit that we are God's children

CHAPTER 1

Genesis 1:1 In the beginning God created the heavens and the earth.

COME FILL THIS PLACE

Job 33:4 The Spirit of God has made me; the breath of the Almighty gives me life.

Proverbs 22:2 Rich and poor have this in common: The Lord is the Maker of them all.

Jeremiah 23:24 "Do not I fill heaven and earth?" declares the Lord.

Isaiah 40:28 Do you not know? Have you not heard? The Lord is the everlasting God, the Creator of the ends of the earth.

Psalm 89:34 I will not violate my covenant or alter what my lips have uttered.

Deuteronomy 31:6 Be strong and courageous. Do not be afraid or terrified because of them, for the Lord your God goes with you; He will never leave you nor forsake you.

Jeremiah 31:3 The Lord appeared to us in the past, saying: "I have loved you with an everlasting love; I have drawn you with unfailing kindness.

1 Peter 5:7 Cast all your anxiety on Him because He cares for you.

Psalm 55:22 Cast your cares on the Lord and He will sustain you; He will never let the righteous be shaken.

Isaiah 2:20 In that day people will throw away to the moles and bats, their idols of silver and idols of gold, which they made to worship.

Exodus 3:11 But Moses said to God, "Who am I that I should go to Pharaoh and bring the Israelites out of Egypt?"

Exodus 4:10-12 Moses said to the Lord, "Pardon your servant, Lord. I have never been eloquent, neither in the past nor since you have spoken to your servant. I am slow of speech and tongue."

Exodus 3:19-22 "But I know that the king of Egypt will not let you go unless a mighty hand compels him. So I will stretch out my hand and strike the Egyptians with all the wonders that I will perform among them. After that, he will let you go. And I will make the Egyptians favorably disposed toward this people, so that when you leave you will not go empty-handed. Every woman is to ask her neighbor and any woman living in her house for articles of silver and gold and for clothing, which you will put on your sons and daughters. And so you will plunder the Egyptians."

Exodus 6:1 Then the Lord said to Moses, "Now you will see what I will do to Pharaoh: Because of my mighty hand he will let them go; because of my mighty hand he will drive them out of his country."

Psalm 139:23 Search me, God, and know my heart; test me and know my anxious thoughts.

Isaiah 55:8-9 For my thoughts are not your thoughts, neither are your ways my ways," declares the Lord. "As the heavens are higher than the earth, so are my ways higher than your ways and my thoughts than your thoughts."

1 Corinthians 2:12 What we have received is not the spirit of the world, but the Spirit who is from God, so that we may understand what God has freely given us.

1 Corinthians 12:15-20 If the foot says, "Because I am not a hand, I am not a part of the body," it is not for this reason any the less a part of the body. And if the ear says, "Because I am not an eye, I am not a part of the body," it is not for this reason any the less a part of the body. If the whole body were an eye, where would the hearing be? If the whole were hearing, where would the sense of smell be? But now God has placed the members, each one of them, in the body, just as He desired. If they were all one member, where would the body be? But now there are many members, but one body.

Mark 12:20-31 "There were seven brothers; and the first took a wife, and died leaving no children. "The second one married her, and died leaving behind no children; and the third likewise; and *so,* all seven left no children. Last of all the woman died also. "In the resurrection, when they rise again, which one's wife will she be? For all seven had married her." Jesus said to them, "Is this not the reason you are mistaken, that you do not understand the Scriptures or the power of God?

"For when they rise from the dead, they neither marry nor are given in marriage, but are like angels in heaven. "But regarding the fact that the dead rise again, have you not read in the book of Moses, in the passage about the burning bush, how God spoke to him, saying, 'I am the God of Abraham, and the God of Isaac, and the God of Jacob'? "He is not the God of the dead, but of the living; you are greatly mistaken."One of the scribes came and heard them arguing, and recognizing that He had answered them well, asked Him, "What commandment is the foremost of all?" Jesus answered, "The foremost is, 'hear, o Israel! The Lord our God is one lord; and you shall love the Lord your God with all your heart, and with all your soul, and with all your mind, and with all your strength.' "The second is this, 'you shall love your neighbor as yourself.' There is no other commandment greater than these."

Colossians 3:12-14 So, as those who have been chosen of God, holy and beloved, put on a heart of compassion, kindness, humility, gentleness and patience; bearing with one another, and forgiving each other, whoever has a complaint against anyone; just as the Lord forgave you, so also should you. Beyond all these things *put on* love, which is the perfect bond of unity.

Luke 10:25-27 And a lawyer stood up and put Him to the test, saying, "Teacher, what shall I do to inherit eternal life?" And He said to him, "What is written in the Law? How does it read to you?" And he answered, "you shall love the Lord your God with all your heart, and with all your soul, and with all your strength, and with all your mind; and your neighbor as yourself."

Luke 18:2-6 "In a certain city there was a judge who did not fear God and did not respect man. "There was a widow in that city, and she kept coming to him, saying, 'Give me legal protection from my opponent.' "For a while he was unwilling; but afterward he said to himself, 'Even though I do not fear God nor respect man, yet because this widow bothers me, I will give her legal protection, otherwise by continually coming she will wear me out.'" And the Lord said, "Hear what the

APPENDIX

unrighteous judge said; now, will not God bring about justice for His elect who cry to Him day and night, and will He delay long over them?

Ephesians 6:18 And pray in the Spirit on all occasions with all kinds of prayers and requests. With this in mind, be alert and always keep on praying for all the Lord's people.

1 Thessalonians 5:17 pray continually,

CHAPTER 2

James 4:2-3 You desire but do not have, so you kill. You covet but you cannot get what you want, so you quarrel and fight. You do not have because you do not ask God. When you ask, you do not receive, because you ask with wrong motives, that you may spend what you get on your pleasures.

Proverbs 22:4 Humility is the fear of the LORD; its wages are riches and honor and life.

Exodus 18:11 Now I know that the LORD is greater than all other gods, for he did this to those who had treated Israel arrogantly."

Psalm 115:3 Our God is in heaven; He does whatever pleases Him.

Psalm 102:12 But you, Lord, sit enthroned forever; your renown endures through all generations.

Psalm 90:2 Before the mountains were born or you brought forth the whole world, form everlasting to everlasting you are God.

Ephesians 1:11 In Him we were also chosen, having been predestined according to the plan of Him who works out everything in conformity with the purpose of His will . . .

Isaiah 55:8-9 For my thoughts are not your thoughts, neither are your ways my ways," declares the Lord. "As the heavens are higher than the earth, so are my ways higher than your ways and my thoughts than your thoughts."

John 8:23 But he continued, "You are from below; I am from above. You are of this world; I am not of this world."

Psalm 113:5-6 Who is like the LORD our God, Who is enthroned on high, Who humbles Himself to behold the things that are in heaven and in the earth?

Genesis 1:3-5 And God said, "Let there be light," and there was light. God saw that the light was good, and he separated the light from the darkness. God called the light "day," and the darkness he called "night." And there was evening, and there was morning—the first day.

Psalm 102:12 But you, Lord, sit enthroned forever; your renown endures through all generations.

Psalm 90:2 Before the mountains were born or you brought forth the whole world, from everlasting to everlasting you are God.

1 John 4:8 Whoever does not love does not know God, because God is love.

1 John 4:16 And so we know and rely on the love God has for us. God is love. Whoever lives in love lives in God, and God in them.

Exodus 3:5-6 Then He said, "Do not come near here; remove your sandals from your feet, for the place on which you are standing is holy ground." He said also, "I am the God of your father, the God of Abraham, the God of Isaac, and the God of Jacob." Then Moses hid his face, for he was afraid to look at God.

1 Samuel 2:2 "There is no one holy like the LORD; there is no one besides you; there is no Rock like our God.

Psalm 99:2-3 Great is the Lord in Zion; He is exalted over all the nations. Let them praise your great and awesome name—He is holy.

Isaiah 6:3 And they were calling to one another: "Holy, holy, holy is the Lord Almighty; the whole earth is full of his glory."

APPENDIX

Revelations 4:8 Each of the four living creatures had six wings and was covered with eyes all around, even under its wings. Day and night they never stop saying: "'Holy, holy, holy is the Lord God Almighty, who was, and is, and is to come."

Psalm 147:5 Great is our Lord and mighty in power; His understanding has no limit.

Acts 15:18 things known from long ago.

Romans 11:33 Oh, the depth of the riches of the wisdom and knowledge of God! How unsearchable His judgments, and His paths beyond tracing out!

1 John 3:20 If our hearts condemn us, we know that God is greater than our hearts, and He knows everything.

Hebrews 4:13 Nothing in all creation is hidden from God's sight. Everything is uncovered and laid bare before the eyes of Him to whom we must give account.

Romans 12:16 Live in harmony with one another. Do not be proud, but be willing to associate with people of low position. Do not be conceited.

Psalm 147:5 Great is our Lord and mighty in power; his understanding has no limit.

Acts 15:18 says the Lord, who does these things', things known from long ago.

Romans 11:33 Oh, the depth of the riches of the wisdom and knowledge of God! How unsearchable his judgments, and his paths beyond tracing out!

1 John 3:20 If our hearts condemn us, we know that God is greater than our hearts, and he knows everything.

Hebrews 4:13 Nothing in all creation is hidden from God's sight. Everything is uncovered and laid bare before the eyes of him to whom we must give account.

Romans 2:16 This will take place on the day when God judges people's secrets through Jesus Christ, as my gospel declares.

COME FILL THIS PLACE

Exodus 34:6 And he passed in front of Moses, proclaiming, "The Lord, the Lord, the compassionate and gracious God, slow to anger, abounding in love and faithfulness,

Deuteronomy 7:9 Know therefore that the Lord your God is God; He is the faithful God, keeping His covenant of love to a thousand generations of those who love Him and keep His commandments.

Revelations 13:4 People worshiped the dragon because he had given authority to the beast, and they also worshiped the beast and asked, "Who is like the beast? Who can wage war against it?"

Malachi 3:6 "I the Lord do not change."

James 1:17 Every good and perfect gift is from above, coming down from the Father of the heavenly lights, who does not change like shifting shadows.

Hebrews 13:8 Jesus Christ is the same yesterday, today, and forever

Galatians 5:22-23 But the fruit of the Spirit is love, joy, peace, patience, kindness, goodness, faithfulness, gentleness, self-control; against such things there is no law.

Matthew 6:7 And when you pray, do not keep on babbling like pagans, for they think they will be heard because of their many words.

Ecclesiastes 11:9 You who are young, be happy while you are young, and let your heart give you joy in the days of your youth. Follow the ways of your heart and whatever your eyes see, but know that for all these things God will bring you into judgment.

Romans 8:26-27 In the same way the Spirit also helps our weakness; for we do not know how to pray as we should, but the Spirit Himself intercedes for us with groanings too deep for words; and He who searches the hearts knows what the mind of the Spirit is, because He intercedes for the saints according to the will of God.

APPENDIX

Ezekiel 28:17 Your heart became proud on account of your beauty, and you corrupted your wisdom because of your splendor. So I threw you to the earth; I made a spectacle of you before kings.

Romans 12:3-8 For through the grace given to me I say to everyone among you not to think more highly of himself than he ought to think; but to think so as to have sound judgment, as God has allotted to each a measure of faith.

Revelation 1:8 "I am the Alpha and the Omega," says the Lord God, "who is, and who was, and who is to come, the Almighty."

Nehemiah 9:6 You alone are the Lord. You made the heavens, even the highest heavens, and all their starry host, the earth and all that is on it, the seas and all that is in them. You give life to everything, and the multitudes of heaven worship you.

John 14:15 If you love me, you will keep my commandments.

Isaiah 46:9 Remember the former things of old; for I am God, and there is no other; I am God, and there is none like me.

CHAPTER 3

Deuteronomy 15:10 Give generously to them and do so without a grudging heart; then because of this the LORD your God will bless you in all your work and in everything you put your hand to.

2 Corinthians 9:11 You will be enriched in every way so that you can be generous on every occasion, and through us your generosity will result in thanksgiving to God.

Malachi 3:10 Bring the whole tithe into the storehouse, that there may be food in my house. Test me in this," says the LORD Almighty, "and see if I will not throw open the floodgates of heaven and pour out so much blessing that there will not be room enough to store it.

Luke 12:22-34 And He said to His disciples, "For this reason I say to you, do not worry about your life, as to what you will eat; nor for your body, as to what you will put on. "For life is more than food, and the body more than clothing. "Consider the ravens, for they neither sow nor reap; they have no storeroom nor barn, and yet God feeds them; how much more valuable you are than the birds!

CHAPTER 4

Proverbs 4:23 Above all else, guard your heart, for everything you do flows from it.

Philippians 2:13 for it is God who works in you to will and to act in order to fulfill his good purpose.

Psalm 145:8 The Lord is gracious and compassionate, slow to anger and rich in love.

James 4:2-3 You desire but do not have, so you kill. You covet but you cannot get what you want, so you quarrel and fight. You do not have because you do not ask God. When you ask, you do not receive, because you ask with wrong motives, that you may spend what you get on your pleasures.

Psalm 139:23-24 Search me, God, and know my heart; test me and know my anxious thoughts. See if there is any offensive way in me, and lead me in the way everlasting.

Ezekiel 36:26 I will give you a new heart and put a new spirit in you; I will remove from you your heart of stone and give you a heart of flesh.

2 Timothy 1:14 Guard the good deposit that was entrusted to you—guard it with the help of the Holy Spirit who lives in us.

1 John 5:14 This is the confidence we have in approaching God: that if we ask anything according to his will, he hears us.

APPENDIX

Philippians 4:6-7 Do not be anxious about anything, but in every situation, by prayer and petition, with thanksgiving, present your requests to God. And the peace of God, which transcends all understanding, will guard your hearts and your minds in Christ Jesus

Deuteronomy 29:9 Carefully follow the terms of this covenant, so that you may prosper in everything you do.

Jeremiah 29:11 For I know the plans I have for you," declares the Lord, "plans to prosper you and not to harm you, plans to give you hope and a future.

Psalm 27:4 One thing I ask from the Lord, this only do I seek: that I may dwell in the house of the Lord all the days of my life, to gaze on the beauty of the Lord and to seek him in his temple.

Psalm 23:4 Even though I walk through the darkest valley, I will fear no evil, for you are with me; your rod and your staff, they comfort me.

Romans 8:28 And we know that in all things God works for the good of those who love him, who have been called according to his purpose.

Philippians 4:19 And my God will meet all your needs according to the riches of his glory in Christ Jesus.

John 14:16 And I will ask the Father, and he will give you another advocate to help you and be with you forever—

Romans 8:38-39 For I am convinced that neither death nor life, neither angels nor demons, neither the present nor the future, nor any powers, neither height nor depth, nor anything else in all creation, will be able to separate us from the love of God that is in Christ Jesus our Lord.

Matthew 18:18-20 (The Message) "What you say to one another is eternal, I mean this. When two of you get together on anything at all on earth and make a prayer of it, my Father in heaven goes into action. And when two or three of you are together because of me, you can be sure that I'll be there."

Ecclesiastes 11:9 You who are young, be happy while you are young, and let your heart give you joy in the days of your youth. Follow the way of your heart and whatever your eyes see, but know that for all these things. God will bring you into judgment.

Isaiah 45:3 I will give you hidden treasures, riches stored in secret places, so that you may know that I am the Lord, the God of Israel, who summons you by name.

Isaiah 45:1-7 "This is what the Lord says to his anointed, to Cyrus, whose right hand I take hold of to subdue nations before him and to strip kings of their armor, to open doors before him so that gates will not be shut: I will go before you and will level the mountains; I will break down gates of bronze and cut through bars of iron. I will give you hidden treasures, riches stored in secret places, so that you may know that I am the Lord, the God of Israel, who summons you by name. For the sake of Jacob my servant, of Israel my chosen, I summon you by name and bestow on you a title of honor, though you do not acknowledge me. I am the Lord, and there is no other; apart from me there is no God. I will strengthen you, though you have not acknowledged me, so that from the rising of the sun to the place of its setting people may know there is none besides me. I am the Lord, and there is no other. I form the light and create darkness, I bring prosperity and create disaster; I, the Lord, do all these things.

Isaiah 45:13 I will raise up Cyrus in my righteousness: I will make all his ways straight. He will rebuild my city and set my exiles free, but not for a price or reward, says the Lord Almighty."

Hebrews 6:17 Because God wanted to make the unchanging nature of his purpose very clear to the heirs of what was promised, he confirmed it with an oath.

Psalm 89:34 I will not violate my covenant or alter what my lips have uttered.

APPENDIX

James 1:17 Every good and perfect gift is from above, coming down from the Father of the heavenly lights, who does not change like shifting shadows.

Romans 2:11 For God does not show favoritism.

Matthew 13:13 This is why I speak to them in parables: "Though seeing, they do not see; though hearing, they do not hear or understand.

Mark 4:22 For whatever is hidden is meant to be disclosed, and whatever is concealed is meant to be brought out into the open.

Luke 12:2-3 There is nothing concealed that will not be disclosed, or hidden that will not be made known. What you have said in the dark will be heard in the daylight, and what you have whispered in the ear in the inner rooms will be proclaimed from the roofs.

CHAPTER 5

Galatians 6:2 Carry each other's burdens, and in this way you will fulfill the law of Christ.

Luke 23:34 "Father, forgive them, for they do not know what they are doing"

CHAPTER 6

Isaiah 55:9 As the heavens are higher than the earth, so are my ways higher than your ways and my thoughts than your thoughts.

Jeremiah 32:17 Ah, Sovereign Lord, you have made the heavens and the earth by your great power and outstretched arm. Nothing is too hard for you.

John 10:27-28 "My sheep listen to my voice; I know them, and they follow me. I give them eternal life, and they shall never perish; no one will snatch them out of my hand."

Zephaniah 3:17 The Lord your God is with you, the Mighty Warrior who saves. He will take great delight in you; in His love he will no longer rebuke you, but will rejoice over you with singing.

John 14:17 The Spirit of truth. The world cannot accept Him, because it neither sees Him nor knows Him. But you know Him, for He lives with you and will be in you.

CHAPTER 7

Romans 1:20 For since the creation of the world God's invisible qualities—His eternal power and divine nature—have been clearly seen, being understood from what has been made, so that people are without excuse.

John 14:6 Jesus answered, "I am the way and the truth and the life. No one comes to the Father except through me.

2 Corinthians 11:14-15 And no wonder, for Satan himself masquerades as an angel of light. It is not surprising, then, if his servants also masquerade as servants of righteousness. Their end will be what their actions deserve.

1 Peter 5:8 Be alert and of sober mind. Your enemy the devil prowls around like a roaring lion looking for someone to devour.

Matthew 6:13 "And lead us not into temptation, but deliver us from the evil one."

John 8:44 You belong to your father, the devil, and you want to carry out your father's desires. He was a murderer from the beginning, not holding to the truth, for there is no truth in him. When he lies, he speaks his native language, for he is a liar and the father of lies.

Revelation 12:10 Then I heard a loud voice in heaven say: "Now have come the salvation and the power and the kingdom of our God, and the authority of his Messiah. For the accuser of our brothers and sisters, who accuses them before our God day and night, has been hurled down.

APPENDIX

1 Thessalonians 3:5 For this reason, when I could stand it no longer, I sent to find out about your faith. I was afraid that in some way the tempter had tempted you and that our labors might have been in vain.

Isaiah 14:12-15 How you have fallen from heaven, morning star, son of the dawn! You have been cast down to the earth, you who once laid low the nations! You said in your heart, "I will ascend to the heavens; I will raise my throne above the stars of God; I will sit enthroned on the mount of assembly, on the utmost heights of Mount Zaphon. I will ascend above the tops of the clouds; I will make myself like the Most High." But you are brought down to the realm of the dead, to the depths of the pit.

Acts 13:10 You are a child of the devil and an enemy of everything that is right! You are full of all kinds of deceit and trickery. Will you never stop perverting the right ways of the Lord?

Ephesians 6:11 Put on the full armor of God, so that you can take your stand against the devil's schemes.

Luke 8:12 Those along the path are the ones who hear, and then the devil comes and takes away the word from their hearts, so that they may not believe and be saved.

Proverbs 4:23 Above all else, guard your heart, for everything you do flows from it.

2 Corinthians 5:10 For we must all appear before the judgment seat of Christ, so that each of us may receive what is due us for the things done while in the body, whether good or bad.

Matthew 6:21 For where your treasure is, there your heart will be also.

Psalm 9:17 The wicked go down to the realm of the dead, all the nations that forget God.

2 Thessalonians 1:9 They will be punished with everlasting destruction and shut out from the presence of the Lord and from the glory of His might.

COME FILL THIS PLACE

Matthew 25:41 "Then he will say to those on his left, 'Depart from me, you who are cursed, into the eternal fire prepared for the devil and his angels.'"

Acts 22:28 Then the commander said, "I had to pay a lot of money for my citizenship." "But I was born a citizen," Paul replied.

Ephesians 6:10-18 Finally, be strong in the Lord and in his mighty power. Put on the full armor of God, so that you can take your stand against the devil's schemes. For our struggle is not against flesh and blood, but against the rulers, against the authorities, against the powers of this dark world and against the spiritual forces of evil in the heavenly realms. Therefore put on the full armor of God, so that when the day of evil comes, you may be able to stand your ground, and after you have done everything, to stand. Stand firm then, with the belt of truth buckled around your waist, with the breastplate of righteousness in place, and with your feet fitted with the readiness that comes from the gospel of peace. In addition to all this, take up the shield of faith, with which you can extinguish all the flaming arrows of the evil one. Take the helmet of salvation and the sword of the Spirit, which is the word of God. And pray in the Spirit on all occasions with all kinds of prayers and requests. With this in mind, be alert and always keep on praying for all the Lord's people.

2 Corinthians 2:11 . . . in order that Satan might not outwit us. For we are not unaware of his schemes.

Galatians 5:22-23 But the fruit of the Spirit is love, joy, peace, patience, kindness, goodness, faithfulness, gentleness, self-control; against such things there is no law. Now those who belong to Christ Jesus have crucified the flesh with its passions and desires.

Psalm 107:8-9 Let them give thanks to the Lord for His unfailing love and His wonderful deeds for mankind, for He satisfies the thirsty and fills the hungry with good things.

APPENDIX

Psalm 36:5-6 Your love, Lord, reaches to the heavens, your faithfulness to the skies.

Matthew 4:1-4 Then Jesus was led by the Spirit into the wilderness to be tempted by the devil. After fasting forty days and forty nights, he was hungry. The tempter came to him and said, "If you are the Son of God, tell these stones to become bread." Jesus answered, "It is written: 'Man shall not live on bread alone, but on every word that comes from the mouth of God.

Hebrews 11:1 Now faith is confidence in what we hope for and assurance about what we do not see.

Isaiah 55:8-9 "For my thoughts are not your thoughts, neither are your ways my ways," declares the Lord. "As the heavens are higher than the earth, so are my ways higher than your ways and my thoughts than your thoughts."

2 Timothy 3:16 All Scripture is God-breathed and is useful for teaching, rebuking, correcting, and training in righteousness.

Luke 12:48 ". . . From everyone who has been given much, much will be demanded; and from the one who has been entrusted with much, much more will be asked."

James 3:13 Who is wise and understanding among you? Let them show it by their good life, by deeds done in the humility that comes from wisdom.

CHAPTER 8

Romans 8:26 In the same way, the Spirit helps us in our weakness. We do not know what we ought to pray for, but the Spirit Himself intercedes for us through wordless groans.

2 Corinthians 1:21-22 Now He who establishes us with you in Christ and anointed us is God, who also sealed us and gave us the Spirit in our hearts as a pledge.

Jude 1:20 But you, dear friends, by building yourselves up in your most holy faith and praying in the Holy Spirit . . .

COME FILL THIS PLACE

Acts 2:4 All of them were filled with the Holy Spirit and began to speak in other tongues as the Spirit enabled them.

Luke 4:1 Jesus, full of the Holy Spirit, left the Jordan and was led by the Spirit into the wilderness.

Genesis 2:18 The Lord God said, "It is not good for the man to be alone. I will make a helper suitable for him."

2 Corinthians 3:17 Now the Lord is the Spirit, and where the Spirit of the Lord is, there is freedom.

Hebrews 11:1 Now faith is confidence in what we hope for and assurance about what we do not see.

James 1:5 If any of you lacks wisdom, you should ask God, who gives generously to all without finding fault, and it will be given to you.

Proverbs 2:6 For the Lord gives wisdom; from His mouth come knowledge and understanding.

Acts 1:8 "But you will receive power when the Holy Spirit comes on you; and you will be my witnesses in Jerusalem, and in all Judea and Samaria, and to the ends of the earth."

2 Timothy 1:7 For the Spirit God gave us does not make us timid, but gives us power, love, and self-discipline.

1 Corinthians 12:4 There are different kinds of gifts, but the same Spirit distributes them.

1 Corinthians 2:11-12 For who knows a person's thoughts except their own spirit within them? In the same way no one knows the thoughts of God except the Spirit of God. What we have received is not the spirit of the world, but the Spirit who is from God, so that we may understand what God has freely given us.

John 16:8 When He comes, He will prove the world to be in the wrong about sin and righteousness and judgment.

John 14:26 But the Advocate, the Holy Spirit, whom the Father will send in my name, will teach you all things and will remind you of everything I have said to you.

John 16:13 But when He, the Spirit of truth, comes, He will guide you into all the truth.

Galatians 5:22-23 But the fruit of the Spirit is love, joy, peace, forbearance, kindness, goodness, faithfulness, gentleness, and self-control. Against such things there is no law.

John 16:7 "But very truly I tell you, it is for your good that I am going away. Unless I go away, the Advocate will not come to you; but if I go, I will send him to you."

John 15:26 "When the Advocate comes, whom I will send to you from the Father—the Spirit of truth who goes out from the Father—He will testify about me."

Romans 8:14 For those who are led by the Spirit of God are the children of God.

1 Corinthians 2:13 This is what we speak, not in words taught us by human wisdom but in words taught by the Spirit, explaining spiritual realities with Spirit-taught words.

Acts 1:1-2 In my former book, Theophilus, I wrote about all that Jesus began to do and to teach until the day He was taken up to heaven, after giving instructions through the Holy Spirit to the apostles He had chosen.

Genesis 6:3 Then the Lord said, "My Spirit will not contend with humans forever, for they are mortal; their days will be a hundred and twenty years."

Acts 8:28-29 And on his way home was sitting in his chariot reading the Book of Isaiah the prophet. The Spirit told Philip, "Go to that chariot and stay near it."

COME FILL THIS PLACE

Romans 8:26 In the same way, the Spirit helps us in our weakness. We do not know what we ought to pray for, but the Spirit himself intercedes for us through wordless groans.

Acts 13:4 The two of them, sent on their way by the Holy Spirit, went down to Seleucia and sailed from there to Cyprus.

Revelations 22:17 The Spirit and the bride say, "Come!" And let the one who hears say, "Come!" Let the one who is thirsty come; and let the one who wishes take the free gift of the water of life.

1 Corinthians 12:11 All these are the work of one and the same Spirit, and He distributes them to each one, just as he determines.

Isaiah 63:10 Yet they rebelled and grieved His Holy Spirit.

Ephesians 4:30 And do not grieve the Holy Spirit of God, with whom you were sealed for the day of redemption.

Romans 9:1 I speak the truth in Christ—I am not lying, my conscience confirms it through the Holy Spirit.

Genesis 1:1 In the beginning God created the heavens and the earth.

Isaiah 11:2 The Spirit of the Lord will rest on him—the Spirit of wisdom and of understanding, the Spirit of counsel and of might, the Spirit of the knowledge and fear of the Lord.

Luke 24:49 "I am going to send you what my Father has promised; but stay in the city until you have been clothed with power from on high."

Acts 2:38 Peter replied, "Repent and be baptized, every one of you, in the name of Jesus Christ for the forgiveness of your sins. And you will receive the gift of the Holy Spirit."

APPENDIX

John 14:16-17 "I will ask the Father, and He will give you another Helper, that He may be with you forever; that is the Spirit of truth, whom the world cannot receive, because it does not see Him or know Him, but you know Him because He abides with you and will be in you.

1 Corinthians 6:19 Do you not know that your bodies are temples of the Holy Spirit, who is in you, whom you have received from God? You are not your own;

Jeremiah 29:11-14 For I know the plans that I have for you,' declares the Lord, 'plans for welfare and not for calamity to give you a future and a hope. Then you will call upon Me and come and pray to Me, and I will listen to you. 'You will seek Me and find Me when you search for Me with all your heart. 'I will be found by you,' declares the Lord, 'and I will restore your fortunes and will gather you from all the nations and from all the places where I have driven you,' declares the Lord, 'and I will bring you back to the place from where I sent you into exile.'

Romans 8:14 For those who are led by the Spirit of God are the children of God.

Ephesians 1:13-14 In Him, you also, after listening to the message of truth, the gospel of your salvation—having also believed, you were sealed in Him with the Holy Spirit of promise, who is given as a pledge of our inheritance, with a view to the redemption of God's own possession, to the praise of His glory.

Romans 8:26-27 In the same way the Spirit also helps our weakness; for we do not know how to pray as we should, but the Spirit Himself intercedes for us with groanings too deep for words; and He who searches the hearts knows what the mind of the Spirit is, because He intercedes for the saints according to the will of God.

1 Corinthians 14:15 So what shall I do? I will pray with my spirit, but I will also pray with my understanding; I will sing with my spirit, but I will also sing with my understanding

Jude 1:20-23 But you, beloved, building yourselves up on your most holy faith, praying in the Holy Spirit, keep yourselves in the love of God, waiting anxiously for the mercy of our Lord Jesus Christ to eternal life. And have mercy on some, who are doubting; save others, snatching them out of the fire; and on some have mercy with fear, hating even the garment polluted by the flesh.

John 16:8 When He comes, He will prove the world to be in the wrong about sin and righteousness and judgment.

Hebrews 2:1-4 We must pay the most careful attention, therefore, to what we have heard, so that we do not drift away. For since the message spoken through angels was binding, and every violation and disobedience received its just punishment, how shall we escape if we ignore so great a salvation? This salvation, which was first announced by the Lord, was confirmed to us by those who heard Him. God also testified to it by signs, wonders, and various miracles, and by gifts of the Holy Spirit distributed according to his will.

2 Corinthians 1:21-22 Now He who establishes us with you in Christ and anointed us is God, who also sealed us and gave us the Spirit in our hearts as a pledge.

CHAPTER 9

James 5:16 Therefore confess your sins to each other and pray for each other so that you may be healed. The prayer of a righteous person is powerful and effective.

1 John 3:22 and receive from him anything we ask, because we keep his commands and do what pleases him.

John 15:7 If you remain in me and my words remain in you, ask whatever you wish, and it will be done for you.

Mathew 5:3-10 Blessed are the poor in spirit, for theirs is the kingdom of heaven. Blessed are those who mourn, for they will be comforted. Blessed are the meek, for they will inherit the earth. Blessed are those who hunger and thirst for righteousness, for they will be filled. Blessed are the merciful, for they will be shown mercy. Blessed are the pure in heart, for they will see God. Blessed are the peacemakers, for they will be called children of God. Blessed are those who are persecuted because of righteousness, for theirs is the kingdom of heaven.

Matthew 5:11 Blessed are you when people insult you, persecute you and falsely say all kinds of evil against you because of me.

Mathew 5:13 You are the salt of the earth. But if the salt loses its saltiness, how can it be made salty again? It is no longer good for anything, except to be thrown out and trampled underfoot.

Mathew 5:14-16 You are the light of the world. A town built on a hill cannot be hidden. Neither do people light a lamp and put it under a bowl. Instead they put it on its stand, and it gives light to everyone in the house. In the same way, let your light shine before others, that they may see your good deeds and glorify your Father in heaven.

Mathew 5:17-19 Do not think that I have come to abolish the Law or the Prophets; I have not come to abolish them but to fulfill them. For truly I tell you, until heaven and earth disappear, not the smallest letter, not the least stroke of a pen, will by any means disappear from the Law until everything is accomplished. Therefore anyone who sets aside one of the least of these commands and teaches others accordingly will be called least in the kingdom of heaven, but whoever practices and teaches these commands will be called great in the kingdom of heaven.

Matthew 6:9-13 "This, then, is how you should pray: 'Our Father in heaven, hallowed be your name, your kingdom come, your will be done, on earth as it is in heaven. Give us today our daily bread. And forgive us our debts, as we also have forgiven our debtors. And lead us not into temptation, but deliver us from the evil one.'"

COME FILL THIS PLACE

Luke 11:2-4 "Father, hallowed be your name, your kingdom come. Give us each day our daily bread. Forgive us our sins, for we also forgive everyone who sins against us. And lead us not into temptation."

Mark 14:36 "Abba, Father," he said, "everything is possible for you. Take this cup from me. Yet not what I will, but what you will."

Proverbs 11:24-25 One person gives freely, yet gains even more; another withholds unduly, but comes to poverty. A generous person will prosper; whoever refreshes others will be refreshed.

Luke 22:42 "Father, if you are willing, take this cup from me; yet not my will, but yours be done."

Matthew 26:39 Going a little farther, he fell with his face to the ground and prayed, "My Father, if it is possible, may this cup be taken from me. Yet not as I will, but as you will."

Psalm 37:4-7 Take delight in the Lord, and He will give you the desires of your heart. Commit your way to the Lord; trust in Him and He will do this. He will make your righteous reward shine like the dawn, your vindication like the noonday sun. Be still before the Lord and wait patiently for Him; do not fret when people succeed in their ways, when they carry out their wicked schemes.

Matthew 6:34 Therefore do not worry about tomorrow, for tomorrow will worry about itself. Each day has enough trouble of its own.

James 4:13 Now listen, you who say, "Today or tomorrow we will go to this or that city, spend a year there, carry on business and make money."

Matthew 6:19-24 Do not store up for yourselves treasures on earth, where moths and vermin destroy, and where thieves break in and steal. But store up for yourselves treasures in heaven, where moths and vermin do not destroy, and where thieves do not break in and steal. For where your treasure is, there your heart will

APPENDIX

be also. "The eye is the lamp of the body. If your eyes are healthy, your whole body will be full of light. But if your eyes are unhealthy, your whole body will be full of darkness. If then the light within you is darkness, how great is that darkness! "No one can serve two masters. Either you will hate the one and love the other, or you will be devoted to the one and despise the other. You cannot serve both God and money.

Matthew 18:21-35 Then Peter came to Jesus and asked, "Lord, how many times shall I forgive my brother or sister who sins against me? Up to seven times?" Jesus answered, "I tell you, not seven times, but seventy-seven times. "Therefore, the kingdom of heaven is like a king who wanted to settle accounts with his servants. As he began the settlement, a man who owed him ten thousand bags of gold was brought to him. Since he was not able to pay, the master ordered that he and his wife and his children and all that he had be sold to repay the debt. "At this the servant fell on his knees before him. 'Be patient with me,' he begged, 'and I will pay back everything.' The servant's master took pity on him, canceled the debt and let him go. "But when that servant went out, he found one of his fellow servants who owed him a hundred silver coins. He grabbed him and began to choke him. 'Pay back what you owe me!' he demanded. "His fellow servant fell to his knees and begged him, 'Be patient with me, and I will pay it back.' "But he refused. Instead, he went off and had the man thrown into prison until he could pay the debt. When the other servants saw what had happened, they were outraged and went and told their master everything that had happened. "Then the master called the servant in. 'You wicked servant,' he said, 'I canceled all that debt of yours because you begged me to. Shouldn't you have had mercy on your fellow servant just as I had on you?' 34 In anger his master handed him over to the jailers to be tortured, until he should pay back all he owed. "This is how my heavenly Father will treat each of you unless you forgive your brother or sister from your heart."

Colossians 3:12-15 Therefore, as God's chosen people, holy and dearly loved, clothe yourselves with compassion, kindness, humility, gentleness and patience.

Bear with each other and forgive one another if any of you has a grievance against someone. Forgive as the Lord forgave you. And over all these virtues put on love, which binds them all together in perfect unity. Let the peace of Christ rule in your hearts, since as members of one body you were called to peace. And be thankful.

James 4:7-8 Submit yourselves, then, to God. Resist the devil, and he will flee from you. Come near to God and he will come near to you. Wash your hands, you sinners, and purify your hearts, you double-minded.

Matthew 4:1-11 Then Jesus was led by the Spirit into the wilderness to be tempted by the devil. After fasting forty days and forty nights, he was hungry. The tempter came to him and said, "If you are the Son of God, tell these stones to become bread." Jesus answered, "It is written: 'Man shall not live on bread alone, but on every word that comes from the mouth of God.'" Then the devil took him to the holy city and had him stand on the highest point of the temple. "If you are the Son of God," he said, "throw yourself down. For it is written: '"He will command his angels concerning you, and they will lift you up in their hands, so that you will not strike your foot against a stone.'" Jesus answered him, "It is also written: 'Do not put the Lord your God to the test.'" Again, the devil took him to a very high mountain and showed him all the kingdoms of the world and their splendor. "All this I will give you," he said, "if you will bow down and worship me." Jesus said to him, "Away from me, Satan! For it is written: 'Worship the Lord your God, and serve him only.'" Then the devil left him, and angels came and attended him.

Romans 8:28 And we know that in all things God works for the good of those who love Him, who have been called according to His purpose.

CHAPTER 10

Deuteronomy 5:24 And you said, "The Lord our God has shown us His glory and His majesty, and we have heard His voice from the fire. Today we have seen that a person can live even if God speaks with them."

APPENDIX

Psalm 50:1 The Mighty One, God, the Lord, speaks and summons the earth from the rising of the sun to where it sets.

Daniel 2:28 But there is a God in heaven who reveals mysteries. He has shown King Nebuchadnezzar what will happen in days to come. Your dream and the visions that passed through your mind as you were lying in bed are these . . .

Ecclesiastes 3:1 There is a time for everything, and a season for every activity under the heavens . . .

2 Peter 3:8 But do not forget this one thing, dear friends: With the Lord a day is like a thousand years, and a thousand years are like a day.

Psalm 139:4 Before a word is on my tongue you, Lord, know it completely.

Job 37:5 God's voice thunders in marvelous ways; He does great things beyond our understanding.

Matthew 7:7-8 Ask and it will be given to you; seek and you will find; knock and the door will be opened to you. For everyone who asks receives; the one who seeks finds; and to the one who knocks, the door will be opened.

Matthew 6:16-34 "When you fast, do not look somber as the hypocrites do, for they disfigure their faces to show others they are fasting. Truly I tell you, they have received their reward in full. But when you fast, put oil on your head and wash your face, so that it will not be obvious to others that you are fasting, but only to your Father, who is unseen; and your Father, who sees what is done in secret, will reward you. "Do not store up for yourselves treasures on earth, where moths and vermin destroy, and where thieves break in and steal. But store up for yourselves treasures in heaven, where moths and vermin do not destroy, and where thieves do not break in and steal. For where your treasure is, there your heart will be also. "The eye is the lamp of the body. If your eyes are healthy, your whole body will be full of light. But if your eyes are unhealthy, your whole body will be full of darkness. If then the light within you is darkness, how great is that darkness! "No one can serve two masters. Either you will hate the one and love the other, or you will be devoted to the one and despise the other. You cannot serve both God and money. "Therefore I tell you, do not worry about your life, what you will eat or drink; or about your body, what you will wear. Is not life more than food, and the body more than clothes? Look at the birds of the air; they do not sow or reap or store away in barns, and yet your heavenly Father feeds them. Are you not much more valuable than they? Can any one of you by worrying add a single hour to your life? "And why do you worry about clothes? See how the flowers of the field grow. They do not labor or spin. Yet I tell you that not even Solomon in all his splendor was dressed like one of these. If that is how God clothes the grass of the field, which is here today and tomorrow is thrown into the fire, will he not much more clothe you—you of little faith? So do not worry, saying, 'What shall we eat?' or 'What shall we drink?' or 'What shall we wear?' For the pagans run after all these things, and your heavenly Father knows that you need them. But seek first his kingdom and his righteousness, and all these things will be given to you as well. Therefore do not worry about tomorrow, for tomorrow will worry about itself. Each day has enough trouble of its own.

Matthew 7:1-5 "Do not judge, or you too will be judged. For in the same way you judge others, you will be judged, and with the measure you use, it will be measured to you. "Why do you look at the speck of sawdust in your brother's eye and pay no attention to the plank in your own eye? How can you say to your brother, 'Let me take the speck out of your eye, when all the time there is a plank in your own eye? You hypocrite, first take the plank out of your own eye, and then you will see clearly to remove the speck from your brother's eye.

Matthew 7:6 Do not give dogs what is sacred; do not throw your pearls to pigs. If you do, they may trample them under their feet, and turn and tear you to pieces.

Proverbs 4:14-15 Don't do as the wicked do, and don't follow the path of evildoers. Don't even think about it; don't go that way. Turn away and keep moving.

APPENDIX

Matthew 10:23 "When you are persecuted in one town, flee to the next. I tell you the truth, the Son of Man will return before you have reached all the towns of Israel."

Matthew 7:9-12 "You parents—if your children ask for a loaf of bread, do you give them a stone instead? Or if they ask for a fish, do you give them a snake? Of course not! So if you sinful people know how to give good gifts to your children, how much more will your heavenly Father give good gifts to those who ask him."

1 John 5:14 This is the confidence we have in approaching God: that if we ask anything according to his will, he hears us.

James 4:3 When you ask, you do not receive, because you ask with wrong motives, that you may spend what you get on your pleasures.

Jeremiah 29:11 For I know the plans I have for you," declares the Lord, "plans to prosper you and not to harm you, plans to give you hope and a future.

Jeremiah 29: 12-14 Then you will call on me and come and pray to me, and I will listen to you. You will seek me and find me when you seek me with all your heart. I will be found by you," declares the Lord, "and will bring you back from captivity. I will gather you from all the nations and places where I have banished you," declares the Lord, "and will bring you back to the place from which I carried you into exile."

1 Corinthians 2:7 No, we declare God's wisdom, a mystery that has been hidden and that God destined for our glory before time began.

James 3:1 No, we declare God's wisdom, a mystery that has been hidden and that God destined for our glory before time began.

John 14:23 Jesus replied, "Anyone who loves me will obey my teaching. My Father will love them, and we will come to them and make our home with them.

Psalm 33:11 But the plans of the Lord stand firm forever, the purposes of his heart through all generations.

Matthew 7:8 For everyone who asks receives; the one who seeks finds; and to the one who knocks, the door will be opened.

Matthew 7:9-12 "Which of you, if your son asks for bread, will give him a stone? Or if he asks for a fish, will give him a snake? If you, then, though you are evil, know how to give good gifts to your children, how much more will your Father in heaven give good gifts to those who ask him! So in everything, do to others what you would have them do to you, for this sums up the Law and the Prophets.

Revelations 3:20 Here I am! I stand at the door and knock. If anyone hears my voice and opens the door, I will come in and eat with that person, and they with me.

ABOUT THE AUTHOR

STACY DIETZ

Stacy has a passion for helping others find what can bring real hope, joy, and peace into their lives. Although she didn't always live a life grounded in faith, Christian faith has now been at the root of what she believes for more than twenty-five years. She strives to help others find ways to integrate faith into everyday living. God made everyone unique, and we are all meant to be valued as well as have a growing, spiritual relationship with Him, no matter where we are in our lives. Stacy's work with her local crisis pregnancy center led her into post-abortion ministry. Teaching post-abortion Bible studies and volunteering for Ramah International, has impacted her life immensely. Within her local church, she has served as a small group leader, youth leader, and in women's mentoring ministry as a teaching coach, prayer team leader, and mentor. Stacy is currently working on continuing her education in the field of psychology, pastoral counseling, and theology.

www.ingramcontent.com/pod-product-compliance
Lightning Source LLC
Chambersburg PA
CBHW052136110526
44591CB00012B/1749